FORTUNE
&
FRIENDSHIP
An
Autobiography

Fortune & Friendship
An Autobiography By
Lawrence Clark Powell

R. R. BOWKER COMPANY, NEW YORK/LONDON, 1968

to
FAY
then
&
now
&
always

ACKNOWLEDGMENTS

Thanks are due to Marian Ellithorpe and to Ellen Cole and her staff for typing help; to John N. Berry III and colleagues for criticism; and to the John Simon Guggenheim Memorial Foundation, and its president, Gordon N. Ray, for material aid.

CONTENTS

FOREWORD

I am writing this in London on my sixtieth birthday, the third of September 1966, at the time and the place chosen to commence this memoir of a man's life. It will be an account of the making of my career as determined by two factors: fortune and friendship. I shall write thankfully of those people—father, mother, and wife, teachers, classmates, colleagues—whose friendship helped me grow up and learn to live socially, usefully, happily. Without them, I could not have done what I did.

I want to write also of my fortune, fate, destiny—call it what you will—that from birth straightway moved me across the continent and back four times in as many years, that sent me around the world at eighteen, abroad to study at twenty-three, to Europe and Asia and around the world again, and to nearly all of the United States. In this life of constant excitement, of seeing, learning, loving, I found that writing and speaking were a means of good health. I had to give out, lest I give out. This was the fortune of character and circumstances, over which I had no control.

Mine has been a fortunate life. Too young for the first World War, too old for the second, I was spared the fate that overtook thousands of other young Americans. I was fortunate also in transcending a life that began recklessly, marked by excesses that would probably have shortened it had it not been my fortune to marry a girl who anchored me, albeit on a long hawser. In that anchorage I achieved self-discipline. Good physical health I owe to another friend of forty years, Henry G. Bieler, M.D., who also believed in me as a writer, from my first clumsy efforts.

Books have been my love from earliest years, first as a reader, then as a seller, next as a custodian, and finally as a writer. Through books I have made friends the world around. This will inevitably be a bookish book, though not removed from life. Books hold quintessential life, are realer than reality, in that they are more lasting than human life.

If my wife was my anchor, books were my life preservers. I found them early, in home and public library and at college. In the Depression they provided a way of life. Once on this way, I never left it, all the way to this my sixty-first year. In the beginning, only my mother foresaw this unlikely salvation beyond the excesses and disharmonies of youth. She saw me as a writer, a bookman, and gave me loving encouragement and support. Her only reproach was that I failed to study Latin—she had learned Latin and Greek in taking her A.B. at Cornell University in 1895—which would have enriched my vocabulary. She was right. I should have, and I finally did, after a fashion, using a Haldeman-Julius "Little Blue Book" as a pony.

When finally I became a librarian, a teacher, a writer, those gay friends of my youth, when encountered in later years, were incredulous. Larry Powell a librarian? It was an unlikely turn of fortune. Sometimes even I wonder how it happened. I conclude that fortune and friendship were responsible.

London seems to me the ideal place to write. I first saw London thirty-five years ago, coming from France on the *Golden Arrow*. It seemed a homecoming. I have returned again and again, in 1933, 1950, 1951, 1957, 1960, and 1963, each time feeling more secure and certain that I had found a well of refreshment and strength. Now in 1966 I draw from it once again, and what I write will surely benefit from the vitality of this ancient environment. We hope to live here part of each year.

The wind is from the southwest, and the smoke from the high stacks of Battersea Power Station streams away in a creamy cloud. I begin to write.

CHILD INTO BOY

Fortune brought me as the third and last son of Hudson River Valley Quaker parents who had met while students at Cornell University. Clark was born in 1900, George in 1901, I five years later, unplanned, my mother told me years later. I was born in Washington, D.C., where my father, G. Harold Powell, was in the Bureau of Plant Industry of the Department of Agriculture. The son of a prominent horticulturist, he was trained in pomology by the great Liberty Hyde Bailey of Cornell. Each winter for the first four years of my life we spent in Southern California at Riverside, where my father was investigating the decay of citrus fruit in transit. The results of his field research led to his being made the general manager of the California Fruit Growers Exchange, the Sunkist cooperative, and in 1911 we moved west for good, taking up residence in South Pasadena. The article on my father in the *Dictionary of American Biography* states that cooperative marketing became a kind of religion for him. His Macmillan book, *Cooperation in Agriculture*, was a standard text for many years.

1

Only a few memories of Washington remain. One is of being awakened one night by my mother and carried to the window to see Halley's comet. Another is of President Theodore Roosevelt riding past our house on Sunday morning en route to Rock Creek Park and waving to us children on the front porch. Still another is of the swallows' nest in a drain pipe at the foot of the retaining wall in front of our house. This latter was verified in 1964 when on a visit to Rachel and Edwin Castagna in Baltimore they drove Fay and me to Washington to check on my story of the swallows' nest. We found the old home at 1867 Park Road, overlooking Rock Creek, and so help me, the retaining wall, the drain pipe—everything but the nest itself. Ed took a picture to prove it.

The gap in years meant that I was never close to my brothers, but neither were they close to one another. We were not a clannish family. I was a frail baby, and in manhood never grew taller than five feet six inches or weighed more than 140 pounds. If I had not learned from Dr. Bieler some rules of good diet, I would have probably succumbed early from careless eating, smoking, and drinking. As it proved, I survived them all. My father died in 1922 at fifty from a heart attack. Clark died in 1938 from an accidental fall, George from illness in 1955. My mother lived until 1957, when she too died of natural causes, short of her eighty-seventh birthday. She was wiry and energetic, with the power of swift recuperation which she passed on to me.

My father was a bull of a man, stocky, affectionate, and magnetic. My outer personality came from him, my inner life from my mother. I looked like her, acted like him. I regretted losing him when I was only fifteen. We had begun to come close. Whenever he was home in the evenings—and this was not often, for he travelled

2

widely for Sunkist and for the government during World War I, when he was Herbert Hoover's first assistant in the Food Administration—on those evenings after dinner, in the beautifully furnished home he and my mother had created in South Pasadena, I would climb on his lap and strike a match to light his rich Havanas, then lie snuggled, breathing the fragrance of tobacco smoke and of his skin. Words were unnecessary.

He and my mother, she told me years later, were emotionally incompatible. She was spiritual, fastidious, and unable to meet his need for physical response and warmth. I believe that he and I would have come increasingly close as I grew to manhood. His death, and later that of my brothers, meant that I had to be nearer to my mother than was good for me. I was good to and for her up to the time of her death, but essentially I was my father's son. She and I never spoke the language of the heart. She helped, supported, and believed in me, and was proud of my eventual success. What did I get from her other than my physical appearance? I suppose a literary and bookish bent, aesthetic taste, and a fondness for tea and toast.

Both parents were generous. My father earned a large salary—$20,000 a year—and spent freely. It was the time when a dollar was worth one dollar. He gave my mother an ample allowance for household expenses. Our home was furnished with antiques and Oriental rugs. He drove a Marmon. We had a Lithuanian cook and a Japanese couple as maid and gardener. Yet I never had much money—my allowance was fifty cents a week in return for chores I did—until I began to earn $8 and more a night as a dance musician. Like my father, I spent freely. His death left my mother without any experience in finance. My brother George, employed in a brokerage house, took charge. The Depression caught him with

3

our mother's capital of $50,000 in risky stocks. All was lost. Her sons and her brother supported my mother until her death.

The Depression was a radical turn of fortune. If it had not wiped us out, I would probably have stayed on in Europe, after finishing my studies in France in 1932, and tried a hand at free-lance writing. Instead I came back broke, then married, and Fay and I started up from the bottom.

To return to books in my childhood and boyhood. The house was full of them. Both parents were readers, my father of Nietzsche and H. G. Wells and Romain Rolland, Gautier and Anatole France—strange mixture —and my mother of Edward Carpenter and the Bhagavad-Gita—she was always delving into Spiritualism, New Thought, and Astrology. They gave me books from childhood on and encouraged me to buy my own—the various series of the Rover Boys, Dave Porter, the Boy Allies, Tom Swift; and later Sax Rohmer and Zane Grey.

I discovered the Public Library in South Pasadena and had a card—its number was 3089—from age six. I was recognized as an avid reader by the librarian, dear deaf old Mrs. Nellie Keith, who waived the rule of two books to one withdrawal and let me take home as many as I could carry. An ability to read rapidly was an asset in my later career. I suppose it came from my compulsive nature. *Do it now*, was my mother's rule of order, and it became mine. In the period between youth and manhood I grew lazy and was content to drink and dream and listen to music. It was a time of economic uncertainty. When eventually I had a steady job as a librarian—as of February 1, 1938—the compulsiveness of boyhood returned, and for the next twenty-eight years I never stopped or slowed down.

In addition to the adventure and mystery books of my

boyhood, I was led to poetry by my mother's love of it and her ability to memorize, for example, the whole of *A Child's Garden of Verses*. How I loved to hear her, in the twilight at bedtime, recite "The Lamplighter" or "Travel" or "Farewell to the Farm." When she died, I formed in the UCLA Library a collection of the *Garden* in her memory, from the first edition of 1884 to the latest of scores of illustrated editions. This was a key book in my life.

Another was that huge anthology, *The Home Book of Verse*, compiled by Burton E. Stevenson, librarian of the Chillicothe (Ohio) Public Library. I still have the copy my mother gave me on my birthday in 1915. My taste in poetry was romantic and sentimental, as my own prose eventually tended to be. Another key book was *Grimm's Fairy Tales*. I liked the violence and the fantasy.

There was music in our home, and it became a lifelong love. We had one of the early Victrolas and many Red Seal records of opera and bel canto. My role was to wind the machine and play recitals for my parents and their guests. Here again I preferred the romantic, the sentimental.

My mother started me early on piano lessons, but I preferred outdoor play or reading to practicing, and I never became a good classical pianist. The best thing George ever did for me was to teach me to play his saxophone. I took to it at once and ended up with three saxophones, a clarinet, and my own college dance orchestra. This gave me money, sociability, travel. I could have made a career of it, for I was a natural show-off and entertainer. The music itself proved too empty, as my taste matured. I discovered Beethoven, read my father's copy of *Jean-Christophe*, and wanted to be a composer. When I found that I wasn't, nor would ever be one, I turned my back on music and never again gave any time to playing, except at occasional parties when the ability to entertain relieved me of having to make small talk.

A passion for the movies lasted about five years, from age seven to twelve. Every Friday night we went to the local five-cent Gem Theater (called the "Germ") to see the latest episode in the Pearl White serial. Saturday mornings I rode in to Los Angeles on the Pacific Electric and was in a balcony seat at Grauman's Million Dollar Theater for the eleven o'clock show, preluded by Jesse Crawford "at the mighty Wurlitzer."

I wrote to my favorite stars—William S. Hart, Douglas Fairbanks, Wallace Reid, Charlie Chaplin, Mary Pickford, Mabel Normand, and the Gish sisters—and pinned up their glossy photographs.

As a boy I was either playing violently out-of-doors or reading indoors, sprawled on my sleeping porch bed, munching a candy bar. A show-off, an extrovert, an organizer and leader, I was monarch of the neighborhood gang, and I led it into so much mischief that my mother used to say that anytime she saw a policeman in the neighborhood, she knew Lawrence had done something to summon him.

Fortunately the South Pasadena policemen were kind men, and of course, my father was influential—at the time of his death, he was being drafted by the Republicans to run for United States Senator from California—and I was never in serious trouble. We fought with green oranges, stole neighbors' tangerines and pomegranates, devilled crabby residents and once stuffed one's mailbox with dog turds. We hitchhiked out to San Marino and played in the freight cars on Henry E. Huntington's siding—one had probably just delivered the *Blue Boy!*—and raided the newly landscaped library grounds for exotic fruits. On the Raymond Hotel course we stole golf balls by rolling them down gopher holes.

We were cruel too, and, finding frogs locked in intercourse, we would smash them to jelly with stones. I had a BB air gun and brought down brother Clark's pet tumbler pigeon and buried it, so that he never knew what became of it. I teased my brothers, and when they descended on me with blood in their eyes, I ran to my mother for protection.

"If you don't do something about that brat," Clark once said to her, "he will end up in San Quentin."

I did, years later, as a member of the Governor's Commission on Prison and Hospital libraries. Clark had died, and I couldn't mail him a card postmarked San Quentin.

I hunted rabbits and squirrels, dove and quail, in the Monterey Hills with rifle and shotgun. I bicycled madly. I celebrated the 4th of July with all kinds of dangerous fireworks. Through it all I bore a charmed life. I never had an accident, was never ill, was never troubled by conscience or repentance. I had a lovely life as a boy, as a youth, as a man, even to this day, and I expect always to have. Fortune was at the zenith on September 3, 1906, when I was born at noon in Garfield Memorial Hospital, name Lawrence Chace Powell. Later, when the boys at school shouted for me to go chase Powell, I changed my name to Clark. This might have offended my grandmother, Marcia Chace Powell, but no, when she died in 1932 at eighty-seven, she left me $1,500. Fortune again.

I loved the outdoors from the summers we spent in a rented cottage at Balboa or a cabin at Big Bear Lake, or weekends in our own cabin in Big Santa Anita Canyon. I roamed the orange groves that stretched east from South Pasadena in a dark green forest clear to Riverside and Redlands and the San Bernardino Mountains. Today the forest is one of tract houses. Together with Pat Kelley, a boyhood friend, we peopled the orange groves with characters based on our reading. We wrote a fantastic play and produced it with neighborhood children in the cast. With our schoolmate Harry Ward Ritchie we founded a grammar school newspaper, the *Marengo Literary Leader*, and my first writing appeared in it, prose sketches of the desert and coyotes, and a Fu Manchu serial called *The Purple Dragon*. I sold evening newspapers at Oneonta Junction. I jerked sodas at Taylor's Drugstore on Huntington Drive and was called the "Chocolate Drop" because I gorged on sweets of that flavor.

In high school I played dance music, was yell leader, and acted the role of Willie Baxter in Booth Tarkington's *Seventeen*. I wanted attention, recognition, the limelight, and I got it, first by mischief and later, when I learned the penalties for unsocial behavior, by more acceptable means. I suppose it is why I am writing now.

The last two summers of high school, 1922 and 1923, were important ones. My father died in February 1922, just before Clark graduated from Berkeley in agriculture and went to work as a foreman on the newly irrigated desert acres in southeastern Kern County being developed by Joseph Di Giorgio, the Sicilian immigrant who had risen from fruit peddler to czar of the United Fruit Company. My father, then in the Department of Agriculture, had befriended peddler Di Giorgio, who never forgot the favor. At the time of his death, my father had an option to buy a large bloc of United Fruit Company stock at a low figure. If he had lived and taken it up, he would have been a millionaire.

Clark brought me to the Di Giorgio ranch that summer of 1922, and there I worked as water boy and at a variety of other ranch tasks, loving the desert heat and the cool evenings. Clark had his own phonograph, and we sat on the screen porch of the bunkhouse and listened to Caruso and Alma Gluck.

A year later the summer started with Pat Kelley and my hitchhiking to San Jose to work in the prune orchards. We slept the first night in a haystack alongside the Southern Pacific right-of-way south of San Jose, and the passing freight trains nearly scared us to death.

No work was to be found. Pat returned home, and I went to work as a dictaphone stenographer in my Uncle Harold Clark's Link-Belt office in San Francisco, living with him in Berkeley and commuting by the Key System ferry. I had taken a typing and dictaphone course in high school and it paid off. That was my first taste of San Francisco. I was there when President Harding died in the Palace Hotel, and I watched the caisson bear the coffin to the station at Third and Townsend. The horses' hooves were muffled. A brass band played Chopin's *Funeral March*. If my father had lived, he would have been Harding's Secretary of Agriculture.

Later that summer I joined Clark again and worked in the canteloupe shed. I also fell in love with a local girl. We swiped watermelons by moonlight, and one Sunday we went to a fandango of *vaqueros* on the Tejon Ranch, high in the Tehachapi mountains.

POETRY, MUSIC AND TRAVEL

In the senior year of high school occurred a change of motivation. Because of two good teachers (the first since Martha Crabtree, my third grade teacher who became a lifelong friend), I took joy in study. The first three years I had been bored and rebellious. In typing class I surreptitiously produced a "newspaper," a scurrilous sheet called *Jo Trout's Daily Pimp Stick*, inciting students to overthrow the principal, John E. Alman, who years later was overthrown, murdered by a disgruntled teacher who at the same time killed the superintendent of schools, another teacher and two secretaries. I was suspended once for slamming a teacher's door so hard that the glass shattered; another time for leading most of the class in hooky for the day. A time I didn't get caught was when another student and I stole a batch of student refund checks and went on a forged spending spree in downtown Los Angeles. I received a C in biology, and failed geometry and French. My day didn't come in French until years later, when I returned with a French doctorate and the same teacher who had flunked me, asked me to speak to her class. I did, in French, about the Burgundian way of preparing snails. The students were bug-eyed, and I never told them she had failed me.

Fortunately, I had Professor Howard L. "Bunny" Wilson as my senior history teacher and Miss Lora B. Evans as teacher of English literature. Both perceived my hunger for learning and life. They fed me, and I thrived, making A's in all subjects and never getting in a single scrape.

Another decisive element was the cementing of friendship with Ward Ritchie, then known as Harry. Although we had grown up together from kindergarten, it was not until this year of 1923–24 that we became the friends we still are, joined in common enterprises these forty-odd years.

Ritchie's father was the owner of a pharmacy in Los Angeles and found it necessary in this particular year for him and his wife to leave South Pasadena and live close to the business. Accordingly Harry Ward came to live with my mother and me and Miss Crabtree in our fourteen-room house on Marengo Avenue. Ritchie and I were in the same classes with Professor Wilson and Miss Evans. He edited the weekly newspaper and the yearbook, and induced me to write for both. He drove a red Buick roadster and we went to and from school together, studied in the evening, wrestled in mock fighting, and platonically shared the same girl. We were unalike in every way. Ritchie was relaxed, I was compulsive; he quiet, I noisy; he gentle, I rough. He was tall, thin, blond; I was short, chunky, dark. But we clicked, in the attraction of opposites. Throughout the years we have never had the faintest of misunderstandings, the credit being his, not mine.

In the fall of 1923, when he was playing tackle on the

11

football team, he broke an arm in a game played at Azusa. I became his chauffeur and factotum, and we were constantly together the rest of the year.

Under each senior's picture in the yearbook, *Copa de Oro*, appeared a descriptive caption, written by Ritchie. Mine read, "The personification of pep, the embodiment of energy, the essence of argumentation."

After graduation I worked as chauffeur for an Alhambra attorney and his wife, and companion to their small son and daughter. I drove a Buick limousine which boasted four-wheel brakes and balloon tires. We travelled throughout California. The mother was a frustrated woman and saw in me a kind of older son.

Time came to go to college. If my father had lived, I would have followed him and my mother to Cornell. Clark left for South Africa to head the Department of Horticulture at Pretoria, and after graduation from Stanford, George went to work for Sunkist in New York State. I was needed at home. Ritchie had decided to go to Occidental College. His parents had returned and he was living at home in their new house on Milan Avenue. He persuaded me to enroll at Occidental and ride back and forth in his new Nash roadster.

I was willing. Occidental was not. My high school grades, prior to my senior year, were too low. My mother and I set out to persuade several of my teachers to raise the grades they had given me. We succeeded in algebra and French, all credit to my mother, for I kept quiet while she pleaded. It was harder in biology, because the teacher had scruples. She lived at Redondo Beach. We made the trip on a Big Red Car of the now vanished Pacific Electric. I don't know how my mother managed to persuade that formidable biologist to raise my grade from C to B. Was it because she displayed her Phi Beta Kappa key, knowing that the teacher also wore one?

Occidental took me. Thirty-one years later my mother was in the Greek Theater when the college gave me an honorary degree of Doctor of Literature. She was eighty-five then. Did she remember the summer days of 1924 when she disregarded her pride and begged those teachers to give her son another chance? I had a good feeling that June night at Occidental, for the college had experienced problems earlier in seeing me through the B.A. In my senior year I had been suspended for a week for unbecoming conduct. More later of that.

So Harry Ward Ritchie and Lawrence Clark Powell set out in September to obtain what was called a Higher Education. Also with us was a grammar and high school-mate, Cornelis Evertse Groenewegen, a strapping Dutchman who had entered the fifth grade at Marengo School when his father had come to California from Holland to engage in the nursery business. Cornelis, called Dutch and later Jim, was then frail and shy and subject to bullying. I took his side, whipped the bullies, and earned the friendship of all the Groenewegens. The father was eventually given the task of propagating trees and shrubs for UCLA's new campus in Westwood, and we met again when I went to work there. George Groenewegen looked like a portrait by Rembrandt. The eucalyptus *viminalis* he raised forty years ago in gallon cans today form a stately row that lines Westwood Boulevard, seventy feet tall, white limbed and fair.

Dutch had outgrown his frailty when we entered Occidental. He stood 6'2" and weighed 200 pounds—an ideal center on the freshman football team. Ritchie's broken arm forbade football, and so he became a high jumper on the track team.

We met another freshman from Franklin High School in Highland Park who played tackle on the team and also ran the mile. We formed a confederacy known as the "Four Musketeers." He was Blair Gordon Newell,

13

who became the sculptor; tall, dark, and handsome, a Pan amongst the college nymphs.

Each of the four was desired by one or more of the four fraternities as a pledge, but no fraternity appeared to want us all. The word was spread that we would pledge only as a group. The fraternities were different: the Chi Rhos were drinkers and playboys; the Sigmas religious and intellectual; the Apes were athletes; the Owls a bit of all, without the religious element. We decided on Owl and Key, but we played the others too. Newell and Groenewegen were wooed by the burly Apes. Groenewegen and Ritchie also appealed to the Sigmas. The Chi Rhos wanted me as a piano player to accompany their "orgies."

We were bid by all four, and when on pledge day we joined with eight other freshmen and walked arm in arm down the eucalyptus-lined drive to the Owl House, the fraternity members rushed out in a body to greet us. I sat down on the piano bench and there I stayed most of my years at Oxy, although when I was elected president in my senior year, I did leave the bench for meals and to preside over the weekly chapter meeting. It was a congenial fraternity and the following year became a chapter of Phi Gamma Delta.

In 1924 Occidental College numbered 500 men and women students and a faculty of about fifty. It was strongly Presbyterian. Daily chapel was compulsory and roll was called. Brought up a Quaker, I paid no attention to Presbyterianism. What I did object to was the unmusical nature of their hymnology. Whenever we rose to sing, I groaned off-key, provoking laughter and frowns from the missionaries' sons and daughters among the student body.

Upon enrolling, I chose history as my major subject and entered two classes, one in ancient history taught by Miss Irene Myers, the plump dean of women; the other in English history taught by lean Dean Robert Glass Cleland. My choice was the result of "Bunny" Wilson who made history live for me. Neither Myers nor Cleland had this power. They droned through textbook courses. They were pompous and pious, and what is worse, dull. Myers disliked my flip answers. Cleland distrusted my unorthodoxy. As a student he had been a member of Owl and Key, and coming down to chapter meeting one Monday night, he entered as I was beating out "Jazz Me, Baby," the front room in a jovial uproar. No, he did not trust me, and later he was my nemesis as the officer who righteously suspended me.

Much later, however, when he had mellowed as the Western Americana research specialist at the Huntington Library and I had mended my ways and written a favorable review of his history of California, we became friends.

Dr. Remsen Du Bois Bird was the energetic young president of the college, devoting most of his time to raising money and to laying the foundations for the distinguished institution Occidental eventually became when it discarded the straitjacket of orthodox religion; and I did not come to know him until my doctoral dissertation on Robinson Jeffers, a son of the college, brought me (and Jeffers) to his warm attention.

The influential teacher of my freshman year was an anachronism at the Occidental of that time. Poet and bohemian, just back from Germany where he had earned a Ph.D. with a dissertation at Marburg on "Rossetti's Poetic Use of Color," Carlyle Ferren MacIntyre was in the first of the four years he lasted at Occidental. Tall, mephistophelean, eccentric, now brutal, now tender, Mac was the most exciting, provocative, stimulating teacher of literature I have ever known. The "Four Musketeers" sat in the back row of his freshman class in comparative literature, at first unconvinced by his way

15

of slouching and wisecracking, talking with his back to the class, while he scrawled on the blackboard. When we talked out loud among ourselves, he came down on us with guillotine ferocity, then sewed our heads back on with a quip. It took him only a week to destroy, then recreate us in his own image. We were his for life.

Not for his personality alone, though it had the quality of Ezra Pound's; but also because of his erudition—he had seemingly read everything in every language; for his taste, keen and catholic; and above all, for his commitment to literature. He taught and lived as a poet, a composite of Meleager, Catullus, Villon, Ben Jonson, Herrick, and Byron. No free verse for him. He despised Whitman and all the moderns. His bohemian mode of life was deceptive. Beneath it was an iron will for work.

Mac lived alone in a cabin on the La Crescenta slope of the San Gabriels, a dozen miles from college, in a dwelling place full of art objects from Europe, of books and music, flowers and cats. He made his own "Prohibition" wine and beer. We were warned never to come without being invited, because of his habit at odd hours of debauching the missionaries' daughters, or so he boasted.

Mac had a way with birds and animals, as well as with girls. And with snakes. A pet king snake, black with gold bands, came to school with him in his pocket, where it usually stayed unless summoned. One day in class, however, when Mac was lecturing on Milton's *Paradise Lost*, the serpent slowly emerged from his pocket, fixed the class with glittering eye, forked its tongue, and proceeded to coil around Mac's neck like a black and gold collar. One girl screamed. Another fainted. Mac rushed from the room with a peal of laughter, and the class dissolved in an uproar.

He was a carpenter and stonemason as well as a poet. He changed our lives, at least Ritchie's, Newell's, and mine. Groenewegen transferred to Stanford in his last two years and has given his life to federal government service.

The three of us were turned toward lives of literature and art by the teaching and example of C. F. MacIntyre, Occidental's lasting gift to us. No gift. We had to pay for it, especially Newell and me, for he was more than suspended in his junior year; he was expelled—a matter of love between him and a freshman girl whose father got through to Dean Cleland. MacIntyre himself was sacked in 1928, but not openly. A trade was arranged with UCLA whereby an unwanted professor there, Dr. Percy Houston, came to Oxy and Mac went to Westwood where he lasted ten years before being kicked upstairs to Berkeley and on out to a free life in Mexico and France.

The second of my great teachers was the man who brought MacIntyre to Occidental and who arranged the face-saving trade, B. F. (for Benjamin Franklin) Stelter, the head of the English Department, a Cornell Ph.D. and authority on Shakespeare and Browning. He was a big blond Teuton, bourgeois in his habits, a most unlikely sponsor and protector of Mac. In his classroom manner Stelter was a witty, iconoclastic lecturer who, while apparently speaking of the Elizabethans and Victorians and their poets, was actually ridiculing Presbyterianism. His course in Browning and later seminars on poetics and Shakespeare prepared me for graduate work, as Mac's courses prepared me for life and literature. They complemented each other. I needed both and fortune provided them, as teachers and lasting friends.

Throughout the college years, I was active as a dance musician, playing mostly with a UCLA group nearly every Friday and Saturday night. I rarely got enough sleep; I ate carelessly, smoked, and drank bootleg liquor and homemade wine. In the following summer vacation I took a messenger job in the Sunkist offices where my father had been chief executive. Was it an unconscious attempt to follow his career? It was a brief one. Over the weekend of the 4th of July our orchestra played at the Orange County Fair. We worked all day Saturday and that night until late, and then learned that we had nowhere to sleep, so we bunked in our cars, and badly. Again on Sunday we played all day and that night. We went home with a hundred dollars apiece; I with a sore throat and a fever. My mother put me to bed and I stayed there for a week, just plain worn out. I never returned to the Sunkist job nor did I seek another.

Later in the summer, as my strength began to come back, another orchestra leader came by to ask if I would join his ship's ensemble on the Dollar Line's round-the-world run. It promised the perfect regime for regaining my health. My mother urged me to go. The *President Harrison* was not due to leave westbound from San Francisco until mid-November, which meant that I would have to leave college for a semester.

And so it was that I made my first world tour, visiting many ports in the course of a four-months' voyage—Honolulu, Kobe, Shanghai, Hong Kong, Manila, Singapore, Penang, Colombo, Port Said, Alexandria, Naples, Genoa, Marseilles, Boston, New York, Havana, Cristobal, Balboa, San Pedro, and back to San Francisco. I had just turned nineteen and was still essentially innocent. The voyage did not corrupt me. I was content to be a spectator. It was an exotic show. I put on weight, especially in Italy where the food was rich and abundant. Genoa's arcades were charming. Marseilles' sidewalk cafes pleased me. We were there at the time the franc was devalued. I remember getting the full treatment in a boulevard barber shop—haircut, shave, shampoo, massage, manicure—all for the sum of fourteen cents including tip.

I kept a diary on the trip, a superficial, perfunctory record of what and where. Introspection did not trouble me, nor did I have much of an eye for other people and their ways. I was still asleep, in spite of all that Mac-Intyre had done to awaken me.

Back at home in the spring of 1926 I kept on with orchestra work instead of returning to college. George had transferred to the San Francisco office of Sunkist Growers and was himself playing weekends with a Stanford orchestra. He urged me to join them and live at his fraternity house on the Stanford campus; and to apply for admission to Stanford in the summer quarter. I also saw my Uncle Harold and he offered to pay my expenses at the University of California if I would come and live with him and his wife Emma, a childless couple. Why I did neither and returned to Occidental in the fall is unclear in my memory. It was not Ritchie's influence, for he planned to spend his third year in the University of the South at Sewanee, Tennessee. I believe it was my orchestra connections and the promise of lucrative work that brought me back south of the Tehachapis.

Late spring and summer of 1926 I was playing at resorts on Big Bear Lake. My knowledge of women was advanced by a series of lively adventures, from all of which I emerged with a whole skin. It was beautiful there in the pine forest around the lake where we had spent several boyhood summers. It was a life of pure physical sensation, with no thought of future or past. I had become a good saxophonist or pianist, as the group demanded, with a large repertory committed to memory, so that I could play without attention to the score, leaving me free to concentrate on the most appealing creature on the dance floor. In my final years at college I used to take required reading with me on dance jobs, prop the book open on the music stand and do homework while continuing to play. I became something of a

19

legend for my double-track mind. Couples would stop to see what I was playing and would find on the stand a copy of the *Oxford Book of English Verse*, open to Wordsworth's "Ode on the Intimation of Immortality," on which I was writing a theme.

Back at Occidental in the fall I took Stelter's course in Browning and MacIntyre's in Meredith and Hardy. In Ritchie's absence, Newell and I drew closer. He had decided to major in art. He would often accompany me to dances where I was playing and line up dates for us at the end of the evening. Again I went short on sleep, ate poorly, smoked and drank too much, and still managed to keep my grades medium high, play in dramatics, debate, and be involved in fraternity activities.

In the summer of 1927, while I was playing in a Hollywood nightclub, my mother's health failed. No doctor was able to improve her condition. George came home, and he and I gave blood transfusions. We engaged a practical nurse. We bought prescription whiskey, and I recall times when the four of us, mother, brother, nurse and I, made merry on a pint. One day I brought home a printed sign, "TRUST IN THE LORD" and hung it at the foot of my mother's four-poster bed. "The Bible adds, 'and do good,' " she said. "Bring me a fresh hot-water bottle."

She grew thinner and weaker and would have died at fifty-seven had not fortune brought Dr. Henry G. Bieler our way. He was a graduate of the University of Cincinnati Medical School, and described himself as a chemical pathologist. By diet, he sought to change the body chemistry so that health returned. There was small hope, he told my brother and me; her liver was nearly gone; but it was worth a try. He put her on milk curd and vegetables in minute quantities, with a teaspoon of whiskey when she had sinking spells. George and I took turns staying up all night with her. A slight improvement occurred. Dr. Bieler wished to place her in his rest home in Altadena, where he could strictly control her treatment. We decided to sell the Marengo Avenue house, and store the furniture. George would return to San Francisco and I go to live in the college dormitory.

I had come to love the old redwood house, built as a U around a wistaria-vined, palm-planted patio, with great live oaks in the front and back yards. I was the last to leave. George had gone. My mother was in the ambulance. I stood tearfully in the patio, where the year before I had buried our fourteen-year-old collie Laird, when I felt a hand on my shoulder. It was Dr. Bieler; the first time, I felt, that he had really recognized me. His blue eyes were tender. "It will be all right," he said. "She will pull through." She did indeed, to live another thirty years.

I lived in Swan Hall that college year of 1927–28, visiting my mother twice a week, until in the spring she was well enough to take a furnished apartment in South Pasadena. My room became a rendezvous for those students who liked music and poetry and a glass of the wine I kept in a padlocked closet. Ritchie had returned for his senior year. I continued the pace of dance music by night and classes and activities by day, and I also fell in love with a pretty Presbyterian whom I sat next to in a class in American literature, given by Professor Guy Thompson. My smoking and drinking shocked her, the daughter of an M.D., and I made it worse by voicing contempt for orthodox physicians. We held for each other the fascination of opposites.

At the start of summer vacation in 1928 I made an effort to work at an outdoor job, joining Gordon Newell on a campus work crew wheeling and pouring cement. A week of it nearly killed me. Reprieve came in the form of a tenor saxophone job on the coastwise *Yale*, San Diego–San Pedro–San Francisco. I enjoyed being at sea again, watching the mountainous coast at day's end, the last light on the peaks of the Santa Lucias. I liked the excitement of the evening's work. I was playing with an excellent ensemble, directed by pianist Marvin Hatley, a classicist who made dance arrangements from *The Well-Tempered Clavier*. The trap drummer, Clinton Williams, was a devotee of the poetry of Conrad Aiken; and after midnight we would lie in our bunks, up in the apex of the bow, and read Aiken aloud. An incongruous thing to do, it led to lifelong friendship with Williams, now Dean of Humanities at San Jose State College, and a deepening of what was to be a lifelong commitment to literature.

We were at sea four nights a week, in port three—the wrong port, San Diego, our sister ship the *Harvard* having the advantage of three San Francisco nights.

I returned to college for my senior year as president of Phi Gamma Delta, rooming at the fraternity house with Robert Donaldson. He was of my same build, so we pooled wardrobes and had twice as many changes of clothes. Why did they elect a musician to the highest office? I suppose because of my self-confidence, assurance, and compulsive way of leading.

At pledge day we swept the campus. After playing at a dance that night I came in late and found the house in turmoil. I happened to have a five gallon jug of red wine in the back of my Chevie, brought it in and shared it with the brothers. We got high and decided to taunt the Sigma House across the street, having taken their hoped-for pledges from them. The night ended in a brawl, with the Phi Gam footballers smiting the frailer Sigmas.

I found myself the next morning on Dean Cleland's worn carpet. "Give me the names of those involved," he demanded. I refused, knowing that the college football team would be decimated. "Resign as president of the house," was his next demand. "If the chapter wants me

22

to," I replied. The chapter refused to accept my resignation, when it learned that I alone had taken the rap for the celebrants. My leadership was stronger than ever, which certainly did not appear to Dean Cleland as quite the Presbyterian thing to happen. My punishment was to be banned from campus for a week.

I stayed at the fraternity house, consoled by messages of cheer from Stelter and Mac. And by Fay, my new-found love—Fay Ellen Shoemaker, a seventeen-year-old freshman. I had met her only the week before, after pledging her brother Norman. We had had one date, consisting of a ride to the beach at Santa Monica and back. Our conversation had consisted mostly of non sequiturs.

One evening toward the end of my week of exile, a fraternity pledge came to the door of my room where I was studying, knocked respectfully and said, "Miss Shoemaker wants to see you."

I went downstairs, incredulous, and found Fay at the door.

"You're not supposed to come here," I said.

"I am here," was her answer.

We went on another long ride, talking in riddles, and have been together, more or less, ever since, these thirty-eight years.

If I had not stayed out of college my sophomore year, I would have graduated in 1928 instead of 1929 and missed Fay forever. Fortune once again.

We went together during my senior and her freshman year. She wore my pin and the fragrance of her long, curly, dark brown hair was on the lapel of all my coats. Our path was blocked in the beginning by Dean Cleland. Fay was the niece of the president of the college's Board of Trustees, the Santa Fe Springs oil man, Alphonzo E. Bell, developer of Bel Air where he and his wife, their two daughters and son lived in the mansion called Capo di Monte. She had grown up in San Francisco and Kansas City, where her father was a court reporter, one of seven children. She was being educated by her aunt and uncle to an eventual society marriage, with two years at Marlborough, Los Angeles' finishing school, and now at Occidental.

Dean Cleland reported to the Bells that their niece was falling into the arms of the college rake. I was summoned to Capo di Monte. When Mr. Bell learned that I was a son of the late G. Harold Powell he warmed. "I was a Sunkist Grower. I remember a speech your father once gave in the Whittier Friends Meeting House. It was on cooperation as God's way for us growers. He was a natural born preacher."

Her aunt's citadel was taken when I sat down at the Steinway and played a tango. Mrs. Bell, a beautiful brunette, put a geranium in her hair and moved to my music. I believe they would have preferred me to be wealthy, but we did become friends for life. My suit was clinched when Fay's mother, Otie Wilkerson Shoemaker, born in the highlands of North Carolina of Norwegian parents and raised in the Mary Austin country of California, came on a visit from Kansas City. She looked me in the eye, and then said, "Be good to her."

Fay had an ample allowance which she spent mostly on clothes. Her wardrobe was a dream of taste and style worn on her slim figure. That old goat MacIntyre never stopped licking his lips and envying me my good fortune.

It was another decisive year. I was in love for the first time with a girl of spirit, tenderness, and warmth. I began to write poetry. And in the spring of 1929 I also experienced an aesthetic awakening that led to changes in my life.

Phi Gamma Delta held a regional chapters conference at the Berkeley house, and as president of the Omega

Kappa chapter I was an official delegate. Upon being expelled from Occidental, Newell had gone to Berkeley to study art and after the conference was over, we held a reunion. He was sharing an apartment on the hills north of campus with a graduate student in physics, and that night they took me to a gathering at the home of Arthur Ryder, the famous professor of Sanscrit. It was a memorable evening of music, poetry, conversation, and moderate drinking. The sparkling dialogue was between Professor Ryder and a young physicist named J. Robert Oppenheimer. Newell beamed as he saw my interest in a new and exciting world outside the Occidental cloisters. That was a kind of watershed evening, after which my life ran in a new direction toward a literary end.

The next day was Sunday. Newell and I stayed in his apartment, reading the poetry of Hardy, playing his friend's records of Stravinsky, De Falla, and Rimsky, eating bread and cheese and drinking red wine. We saw the sun down in the Golden Gate, as we pledged eternal friendship. "I am going to be a sculptor," Newell declared, "you be a poet." It came somewhat to pass, although I soon switched to prose. Today Gordon Newell is one of the few sculptors working heroically in granite.

Back in Los Angeles I began to buy classical records and to study pipe organ. I took fewer dance engagements, as they had begun to bore me and also prevented me from being with Fay. I graduated from Occidental short of honors and the Phi Beta Kappa key Stelter wanted me to have. He scolded Fay one evening when we called on him.

"Larry would have had his key if you hadn't come along."

She stuck her tongue out at him and pretended to grieve. Stelter pronounced a blessing on us both.

The key came later, years later, when I was made an

honorary member of Phi Beta Kappa when the University of California Riverside's campus received a charter. The actual key I wore was the one I found among my mother's jewelry after her death. Dr. Stelter too was dead by then, alas, and so he never knew. Fay was present, however, and she remembered.

Now it was Ritchie's influence that began anew to change my life. Upon graduating in 1928 he had begun to study Law, but gave it up after chancing on T. J. Cobden-Sanderson's diary and determining likewise to become a fine printer. At the Frank Wiggins Trade School he learned the rudiments of the craft, acquired type and a press and set up shop and studio in the Abbey San Encino, a kind of cooperative artists' complex, headed by Master Printer Clyde Browne.

By day, Ritchie worked as shipping clerk at Vroman's Bookstore in Pasadena, and when in the fall of 1929 he was promoted to sales clerk, he suggested that I take his job in the shipping room. And so after graduation I entered the book world. I also shared his studio in the Arroyo Seco and continued to study on the Abbey's pipe organ. I had given up dance music altogether by this time, and following Ritchie's example, I had begun to collect books of poetry and *belles-lettres*.

Fay was back at Occidental for her sophomore year. We were together every possible hour. In the fall I had a physical collapse and I went to Dr. Bieler. He warned me against the use of tobacco and alcohol and lack of sleep, put me on a strict diet and said it would take a few months to regain my strength. In the spring of 1930 I returned to Occidental as an assistant in English under Dr. Stelter, intending to get a teaching certificate.

The Vroman interlude had disillusioned me. I sought literature and found business. The manager had no interest in the contents of books. He forbade me to read on company time and was angry when instead of promptly delivering a copy of the newly published Florence edition of *Lady Chatterley's Lover*, I parked the truck and spent the afternoon reading the book. I was fired. My time didn't come until years later when the same manager, Leslie Hood, asked me to write a history of Vroman's for the opening of their new store. Although I didn't know it at the time, the Vroman experience taught me much that proved useful in the buying and processing of large amounts of books. Business methods and literature could be wed, I learned later as the administrator of a large library.

At Occidental I enjoyed Stelter's Shakespeare seminar, but MacIntyre was two years gone, and the required education courses were nonsense. Ritchie had introduced me to the poetry of Robinson Jeffers, and a subsequent visit to Newell in Carmel, where he had a wood-carving studio, revealed the magnificent setting of Jeffers' work. I wanted to write a dissertation on the poet. But where? No American university would accept work on a living writer. Stelter urged me to go abroad.

Fay's sorority sister, Mary Frances Kennedy, had married Alfred Young Fisher and gone to live in Dijon where Fisher was taking his doctorate at the university. Fay wrote and Mary Frances replied, urging me to come there where Professor Georges Connes, head of the English Department, was partial to contemporary literature and where living costs were low and one was removed from the cultural distractions of Paris.

My mother was well recovered and living alone in a villa on the slopes of the Monterey Hills in South Pasadena, and she was enthusiastic about my plan.

It was also strengthened by Fay's intention to travel in Europe that summer with her cousin Minnewa Bell, and she and I foresaw a reunion in Paris. To make it complete, Ritchie intended to spend the year in Paris, apprenticed to F. L. Schmied, the master printer.

The spring went by in a dream. I had "discovered" Beethoven. I wrote poetry to Fay. We walked in the Eagle Rock hills and climbed to the top of the Rock at sunset. We were with Ritchie evenings or with Mac-Intyre at his cabin, where I had begun to make a type-script of his lyrics to take with me. His only objection to my plan was that I was headed for France not Germany, where he had studied. "Goddam Frogs," he growled, "their women will give you the pox." Stelter approved of my attention to Jeffers, an Occidental graduate ignored by his alma mater. Dean Cleland disapproved of Jeffers' anti-Christian philosophy, and later wrote to me that although he recognized Jeffers' genius, he wished to God he had put it to better use.

On the press in the Abbey, Ritchie printed Mac-Intyre's first book of poems, *The Brimming Cup*. I reviewed it in the college newspaper, and also had two letters printed in the *Saturday Review of Literature* in a controversy with Louis Untermeyer over D. H. Law-rence. I was reading and collecting Lawrence's books, starting on the road that would lead eventually to friendship with Frieda Lawrence.

Gordon Newell was married to the beautiful blonde Gloria Stuart, a girl he had met at Berkeley; and I had made such progress on the pipe organ as to enable me to play the service at their wedding in the Episcopal Church in Santa Monica. Neither of them recognized my choice of wedding march. It was the heroic middle section in the *marcia funebre* of Beethoven's *Eroica Symphony*.

My health returned under the strict Bieler regime. Fay neither smoked nor drank and gladly followed my diet. Love, books, poetry, music, friendship and fortune, were mine in that halcyon spring, as I prepared to sail for Le Havre by French Line freighter through the Panama Canal and be rejoined with Fay in Paris. It was a fair prospect as I approached my twenty-fourth year. My capital consisted of $400 received from the sale of my Chevie. We were blissfully ignorant of the Depression which had begun with the stock market crash of the previous October.

LA BELLE JEUNESSE

I boarded the M. S. *Orégon* of the Compagnie Générale Transatlantique on Bastille Day, 1930, for the month-long voyage, with one call at the Atlantic end of the Panama Canal. My baggage consisted of a suitcase of clothes, one of books, and a portable typewriter with a French keyboard. The books included the works of Robinson Jeffers, Browning, Hardy, Shakespeare, *Aristotle's Poetics* by Lane Cooper, Stelter's Cornell master, *Milton's Prosody* by Robert Bridges, Mark Van Doren's anthology of world poetry, the *Oxford Book of English Verse, Lord Jim, Moby Dick, A Farewell to Arms, The Rainbow,* and a dictionary.

On the halcyon voyage I typed MacIntyre's poems from the manuscript he had lent me, and began to annotate Jeffers' poetry which, since the trip to Carmel, had impressed me as our greatest since Whitman. At the back of my mind was the thought of reunion with Fay. We had ended the school year with a few weekends at the Bells' sombre redwood house on Balboa Bay, the two of us, very much in love and also worried about the

future and what life held for us. I sensed in her a strong
maternal instinct, a wish to marry and raise a family, and
she barely nineteen, whereas I felt reborn and eager to
explore the new world music and art were revealing
to me.

She was on the dock when we arrived in Le Havre,
ran up the gangplank, and we met in a long kiss, to the
delight of passengers and dock workers. On the boat
train to Paris we sat close together. She was more beautiful than ever, wearing a dark blue silk suit and black
alligator pumps, a saucy Rome hat, and my Phi Gam pin
on a thin gold chain around her neck.

Paris was huge and confusing. Neither of us spoke
French. We were troubled by uncertainty. I believed
that she should return for three more years of college,
joining me in the summers. She wanted to stay, believing
that if we married, her aunt would support us until I
earned my degree. My $400 would not keep us for long
and I did not know what my mother would send me if I
married. We had never discussed it, but I knew she
believed Fay to be too immature. And so we parted one
morning early in September at the Gare St. Lazare, from
where the boat train left for Cherbourg. It was the most
painful moment of my life. I was racked by ambivalent
feelings. Three years passed before we met again.

I moved into the Hotel Crystal with Ritchie, and that
first night he saw that I drank *vin mousseux* until I
passed out. I slept till noon. He was fond of Fay, but he
too thought her too young for marriage. Ritchie had
fallen in love with a Hungarian girl, or was she Danish,
and was writing poetry for the first time in his life. Not
to be topped, I began a novel, based on the jazz years.
Each afternoon in the Luxembourg Gardens, I rented an
iron chair and wrote on a pad in my lap. At *apéritif* time
at the nearby Deux Magots or Flore, we read aloud our
work in progress. Later we had sandwiches of ham,

Gruyère, or *choucroute garnie* at Brasserie Lipp, where we saw Hemingway hobnobbing with American journalists. I was too shy to ask him to autograph my copy of his *Farewell to Arms*. Paris began to sort itself out. I no longer felt lost, as I had upon arrival. I began to understand and to speak the language.

One day late in September I took the 11:30 *rapide* from Gare de Lyon and went to seek my fortune in Dijon, ancient capital of the Duchy of Burgundy, 200 miles southeast of Paris. Ritchie saw me off.

I lived in the Pension Rigoulot, 14, Rue du Petit-Potet, where the Fishers had been since the previous year. Mary Frances Fisher I had known at college. She was tall, stylish, soft-spoken, kind. Al was new to me. I saw him as the reincarnation of Shelley, even before I knew that he was a poet. He was tall and strong, with blue eyes, pointed nose, and curly blond hair, and he wore a baggy suit of black corduroy. I came to be a kind of younger brother to them for the year and a half we lived under the same roof.

Fisher took me straightway to the Faculty of Letters where he was serving as Lecteur d'Anglais and introduced me to his *maître*, M. Georges Connes, the chairman of English studies, a blond from the Rouergue, built like a blacksmith, the son-in-law of the Sorbonne's Emile Légouis, dean of English scholars in France. Connes had written his Paris dissertation on "La Pensée de H. G. Wells," which is why M. F. had written to me of his disposition to favor contemporary literature.

"So you want to write on Robinson Jeffers?" he said to me. "Very well. Compose an essay giving your reasons why you think him important." He turned away and I did not see him again for two months, at which time I returned with a fifty-page *étude* on Jeffers' poetry. A week later Connes returned it to me with a single sentence written in blue pencil across the first page, "From your account of him, R. J. is well worth writing a book about, and you very well capable of writing it. G. C."

In the meantime I had enrolled in the curriculum for foreign students, studying French language and literature, with lectures on the Symbolists given by the Dean, Pierre Trahard, and lectures on Burgundian folklore by Gaston Roupnel, an eagle-beaked antiquary and novelist, the author of *Nono*, a tale of the Burgundian earth and its vines.

The talking movies were an aid to learning French. René Clair's *Sous les Toits de Paris* and *Le Million* were enchanting, and I went five nights in a row to Charlie Chaplin's *Les Lumières de la Ville*, until I could whistle most of the musical score—and still can.

The Fishers and I were the only Americans in Dijon. I learned French rapidly, and though I never succeeded in speaking it purely, I was eventually taken for an Alsatian. I had let my beard grow, wore corduroys, smoked *Gauloise bleus*, and steeped myself in *la vie française*, including an affair with a French medical student's wife, which ended the day we were drinking in the café and he produced a scalpel and asked me to test its blade with my thumb.

All the while I was reading Jeffers with attention to the details of his lyrics and narratives and their local settings, at the same time following leads by Fisher to other modern works which would throw light on Jeffers' tragic view of life. Krutch's *The Modern Temper*, Unamuno's *The Tragic Sense of Life*, Spengler's *Decline and Fall of the West*, Jeans and Eddington and Whitehead—these I ordered from Brentano's in Paris, and also the works of Shelley, Byron and Wordsworth, when I discovered the influence they had had on the early Jeffers. I had not been able to find Jeffers' first two volumes, the rare *Flagons and Apples*

(1912) and *Californians* (1916), and so from copies
borrowed from Herbert Klein in Berlin, who had
written an Occidental thesis on Jeffers under Stelter the
year we were both teaching assistants, I laboriously
made typescripts for myself. On my wall I pinned up
U.S. Topographic Survey quadrangles of the Big Sur
country, on which I located the action of Jeffers' narratives and the settings of his lyrics. Eventually the map in
my dissertation was drawn by M. F. The California
landscape appeared cameo-clear to me, seen from
Burgundy as through the wrong end of a telescope.

Fisher was writing his dissertation on Shakespearean
comedy, and I offered to make the final copy to go to
the printer. Ours was a symbiotic relationship. From
Fisher I learned how to construct a thesis from the mass
of data I was accumulating. He was kind, critical, patient, a born teacher. I in turn, in addition to being his
typist, gave him insight into the jazz age. He was a
minister's son and had never lived in the sense that I had.
M. F. was the only woman he had ever known. She
encouraged me to keep on with my jazz novel and to
write short stories, and she herself was beginning to
write the pieces that were eventually to bring her fame
as a writer on gastronomy and human foibles. Her book
The Gastronomical Me tells her story of our Dijon days.
Memorable were the winter evenings the three of us
spent in their chambers, reading aloud from work in
progress, sipping burgundy and nibbling cheese and
crackers. Fisher was writing an epic poem, mysteriously
called "The Ghost in the Underblows," which eventually, after our return to California, I persuaded him to
let me type out and have published by private subscription in 1940, and printed by Ritchie.

My best French friend was Jean Matruchot, professor
of English in the Lycée Carnot, the school Henry Miller
wrote about in *Tropic of Cancer*. In 1931 Miller and I

were in Dijon at the same time, and Matruchot introduced us one day in passing. Neither impressed the other. It was ten years later in California that we remet and became friends.

Matruchot was twenty years older than I, stocky, gruff, a misanthropic bachelor, disillusioned by World War I in which because of bad eyesight his role had been that of interpreter for the American army billeted near Dijon. Unlike Connes whose English was English English, Matruchot spoke fluent and idiomatic American English and was an ardent student of our literature from Brockden Brown to Hemingway.

The reason he took to me, according to Fisher, was that I was the spitting image of his younger brother Henri, a sculptor who had been apprenticed to Rodin, and who had been killed on the last day of the war, November 10, 1918, by a direct shell hit which had blown him to irretrievable smithereens. First sight of me, bearded and corduroyed, had given Matruchot a profound shock. We came to be friends, exchanging conversation for two hours twice a week, once in English, once in French. With his help I translated some of Jeffers, an exercise which improved my English almost as much as it did my French.

Fay and I corresponded, though without satisfaction. She wrote me how unhappy she was, which made me ashamed to dwell on the joys I was experiencing as a Frenchman. My life was devoted to studying, bicycling, enjoying several women in turn, and going up to Paris or into the deep countryside. I was learning to drink abstemiously. I was unaware of the creeping economic paralysis at home. Living costs in Dijon were low. For $1.20 a day I had room and three meals. There was no tuition to pay at the university. When my $400 was gone, my Uncle Harold sent as much again. As his only nephew, I was like a son to him, and he extended his tolerance, if not comprehension, to include a scabrous free verse poem I foolishly sent back home for family reading. Dr. Bieler and I had become regular correspondents, and in his letters he usually tucked a $5 bill. He hoped to come over in a year or two.

In the summer of 1931 M. F. went home for a visit, and Al and I were together day and night, walking, talking, studying, drinking, smoking, a relationship like the one Ritchie and I knew the year he lived at our home. Ritchie had returned home via the printers of London and had set up his own press in the garage of the Milan Avenue home. We corresponded regularly. Newell was living in Hollywood. MacIntyre sent obscene ballads about the perils of French women. Apparently he had once been poxed by one.

Fisher and I drank our noon *apéritif* at the café on the Place du Théatre, along the route taken by the prostitutes on their weekly visit to the medical inspector, and we would banter with the girls as they passed. "When are you coming to see us?" they asked. One night we did, making the rounds of several whorehouses, buying a few drinks at each one but no more. At the last stop I was high. Sitting down at the piano in the parlor, I began to play and never stopped till daylight showed at the window. The girls were enchanted. Fisher danced with each in turn, and they ended by giving us breakfast. The Madame offered me a job, in return for free meals. I declined.

Later that summer I went to Berlin and stayed with Herbert Klein who was working for the *Chicago Tribune's* correspondent, Sigrid Schultz. From the Trib's upper windows on Unter den Linden we looked down on a torchlight parade of goose-stepping, brownshirted storm troopers, then followed them to the Sports Palace and heard Adolf Hitler scream and rave to a responsive house of his followers. Klein, a Jew and a

Communist sympathizer, foresaw the cataclysm and quit Germany the day after Hitler came to power two years later. That visit was of prime importance to the completion of my studies, for we discussed Jeffers in every free hour.

That fall saw Fisher successfully defend his Shakespeare thesis in public examination called the *soutenance*. Professor Emile Légouis came from Paris to lead the examiners. It was a preview of what I could expect a year hence when my turn came.

The end followed to our life in the Rue du Petit-Potet. The Fishers left for Strasbourg and more postgraduate study. The Rigoulots closed the *pension*, although I was able to rent the Fishers' two-room apartment from the new landlord. I hated cooking. My mother came to the rescue. I met her ship in Le Havre and she kept house for me for the following year.

In the spring of 1932, however, she was in London to visit Clark, on sick leave from South Africa, and I went to the Riviera to a fishing village near Nice where the Fishers had gone from Strasbourg prior to returning to California. There at the Pension de la Plage I began the actual composition of my thesis, and although I received no specific help from Fisher—he was in a withdrawn and introspective state—I was sustained by his mere presence. M. F. and I came close with not the least touch and few words. It was beautiful there on the shore between the lavender hills and the blue sea. I wrote every morning, walked on the beach or in the hills in the afternoon, and spent the evenings reading aloud with the Fishers.

My mother and I rejoined forces for the summer in Dijon, an idyllic one described by her in the chapter "Summertime in Burgundy" in her book *The Quiet Side of Europe*. Dr. Bieler made his first trip to Europe and paid my expenses to be his guide for a week in Paris. It was a time of walking and talking the clock around. I read him parts of the thesis and also chapters from the novel which I kept slowly advancing, and he encouraged me to persist in writing.

The thesis was finally finished and I saw it through press in the shop where Joyce's *Ulysses* and Hemingway's first book had been printed. I read proof in the tiny Café du Midi in the Rue Monge above which the poet Crébillon had been born in 1671. D. H. Lawrence's letters had just been published, and I was absorbed also in reading them, some of the most beautiful of all his prose.

The time for a *soutenance* is never fixed far ahead, thus humanely sparing the candidate the agonies of anticipation. I only knew that it would be held after the term began on October 15. I was distracted by an interlude which briefly evoked my past as a jazz musician. In a magazine published in Brussels called *Le Jazz Hot* I had read an article by a Belgian, so full of errors that I wrote a corrective letter to the editor, adding some reminiscences of my own and giving my new Dijon address, 29, Rue Crébillon.

Along about the 23rd of October there was a knock on the door and I opened it to a gangling young Frenchman who said he had read my letter in *Le Jazz Hot*. He asked if I would come to his home and improvise with his own amateur band. Where? At Chaumont, in the Champagne country north of Dijon. When? Now. His car was below. It was indeed, a chauffeur-driven, dark red Renault. I packed an overnight bag and away we went. He proved to be the son of a rich vintner, the home a chateau, the piano a Pleyel painted *à la mode de Fragonard*. I played it into the floor, as his amateur group blew sour notes. Food and drink were plentiful. We played most of the night. I found it a welcome release from tension.

Back in Dijon the next day, I received a notice from

the secretary of the Faculty that the *soutenance* of M. Powell would be held at 14:30 o'clock on Thursday, 29 October. I was too relaxed to worry. Matruchot helped me polish the half-hour oral précis with which I was required to open the examination. Chief examiner was to be the venerable Charles Cestre, dean of American studies in the Sorbonne, a native of Burgundy, who had commenced his education long years before at Lycée Carnot. Others were Dean Trahard, comparative literature Professor Charles Lambert, and of course M. Connes.

So there I sat, facing that formidable jury, in my moment of truth. In addition to my printed thesis on Jeffers, I was required to defend two additional topics chosen by me, one "La Thème de l'inceste dans l'oeuvre de Byron et Shelley," the other "La Côte Pacifique dans l'oeuvre de Walt Whitman." I was prepared on all three, and I had been coached by Matruchot to encourage Professor Cestre and Dean Trahard to reveal to the audience their erudition, rather than expose my lack of it. Audience? A roomful of students, professors, the Rigoulot family, two of my favorite café waiters, my mother, Matruchot, and—so help me God—the Madame, if not the girls, of the whorehouse where I had played the piano till dawn. The local paper had announced the time and place of my public examination. When I saw her in the farthest back row and caught a kiss blown to me, I knew it was going to be all right.

And it was. Again Fortune smiled. I found my French fluent, although my accent brought to the Dean's face the expression of a man passing a peach pit. My *maître,* Georges Connes, as chairman of the examiners, favored me and encouraged both Cestre and Trahard to hold forth at length, the former on the beauty of the sea fog at Carmel (he had taught a year at Stanford) and Trahard on incest in the Bible, which theme he proceeded wickedly to expand upon. I kept quiet.

The *soutenance* lasted three hours. When I returned to the room, after the examiners had balloted, I was greeted by Connes with a Gallic embrace. The audience cheered, and the Madame made a discreet exit out the back door. I received the degree with *mention très honorable,* the equivalent of *summa cum laude.*

That night the Connes entertained me and my mother, Cestre and Matruchot, at a gala dinner at their home. Food and wine, brandy and talk were rich and abundant.

Under the heading "La Vie Universitaire," the *Progrès de la Côte d'Or* printed an article on my examination, which concluded:

> "Il y a sans doute quelque chose de paradoxal a ce que, de 10.000 kilomètres et plus, un jeune californien vienne de plus beau pays du monde écrire et soutenir à Dijon une thèse sur un poète californien; notre libéralisme, sinon notre rayonnement, explique sans doute ce paradoxe. M. Cestre s'est plu à louer, en la thèse de M. Powell, le livre le plus complet et le plus exact, qui ait eté écrit à l'heure actuelle sur un très grand poète, que tous deux tiennent pour le plus grand que l'Amérique ait produit depuis Walt Whitman; livre, de plus, écrit par un artiste sur un artiste."

Back home the Depression was in full flower. George wrote that my mother's income was down to $40 a month and not to expect any more funds. Uncle Harold was having his troubles. Fay and I had drifted apart. I had heard from Dr. Bieler that she had left school and married.

My mother and I took stock of our affairs. We had $16 between us. On the very next day the wheel of Fortune came round. The postman delivered a registered letter from the National City Bank of New York. It contained a draft on the Société Générale's Dijon branch for $1,500, a legacy from Grandmother Powell. We took the $16 and went to Racouchot's Aux Trois Faisans, Dijon's three-star restaurant, and had a great meal with a bottle of 1929 Chambertin.

A trip to Switzerland followed and winter on the Riviera and spring in Italy, then on to England in the summer. My brothers, who had also received $1,500 each, gave theirs to my mother, enabling her to stay in Europe for another year.

She urged me to remain in London and continue to write. I had begun the novel in a third draft. It was drudgery. Would I ever master the language? I was squiring an English girl, a commercial artist, and it was my mother's hope that I would marry her and remain in England. I still wanted to be free.

And I was homesick for California. The Jeffers had invited me to visit them in Carmel. Jake Zeitlin and Ritchie had proposed an American edition of my thesis.

Seventy-five dollars bought a third-class berth in the *Majestic* of the White Star Line. The only disadvantage was that the berth was over the propellers, and the stern of the huge ship shivered and shook throughout the crossing. A Cornell student dance band played in third-class, and I sat in with them in a recall of old times.

UP FROM THE BOTTOM

In New York, I was met at the dock by Ross Park, a former singer with my orchestra, now business manager for Fred Waring's Pennsylvanians. We drove to Riverdale-on-Hudson, where I stayed with my father's younger sister, Mabel Satterlee, wealthy widow of a society doctor. She had spent some time with my mother and me in Italy and England. Recalling how my father had once given her a trip to Europe before she had married, she invited me to stay with her in Riverdale. It was a large house on wooded grounds, sloping to the Hudson River. I was happy there for a week, writing on the interminable novel and reading Lawrence's poetry and Havelock Ellis's *The Dance of Life*. In the long twilights we saw myriad fireflies over the lawn. Another element in my willingness to tarry was that I was broke. When I mentioned this to Aunt Mabel, her face wizened, and I learned for the first time that very rich people can also be very stingy. She grudgingly loaned me $75, requesting payment as soon as I arrived in California. It was a dozen years before I was able to repay her. She never stopped dunning me.

After I had repaid her, however, we became friends, until she lost her mind and finally died at eighty-six in a Florida hospital, cared for by an adopted son.

My friend Herbert Klein was back in New York in newspaper work. Through him I met Ernest Bloch, the Swiss-American composer at a private performance of his newest Jewish sacred music. After the beauty of Paris and the dignity of London, New York's dirt and noise and rush appalled me. I went to Chicago by a night train, sitting up in a grimy chair car in back of the *Commodore Vanderbilt's* powerful steam engine. A former Occidental philosophy professor, Merritt H. Moore, was teaching at the University of Chicago and we had corresponded while I was in France. He and his wife Jean gave me bed and board long enough for us to visit Chicago's World's Fair.

Then I rode all the way to California in a Ford V-8 roadster with a student heading home, and in Berkeley I stayed with my Aunt Marian, my mother's sister, who taught art at San Francisco State College and was herself a talented painter. With my beautiful blonde cousin, Carolyn, nineteen, and newly in love with a Berkeley pre-med student, I walked on the golden hills, read poetry, and went dancing one night at the Mark Hopkins. I spent one entire day on the Bay ferries, crossing to the city and over to Sausalito. In front of the San Francisco Stock Exchange Building I saw Ralph Stackpole's colossal stone figures on which Gordon Newell had worked as an apprentice.

And then I went by Greyhound bus to Monterey and Carmel and my long anticipated rendezvous with Robinson Jeffers. He and his wife, Una, were kind to me. I stayed a week, exploring the Big Sur, and gathering material for a revised edition of my thesis. Jake Zeitlin, the Los Angeles bookseller, planned to issue it from his newly founded Primavera Press, a regional venture in which his partners were Ward Ritchie, Phil Townsend Hanna, editor of the Auto Club's monthly *Westways*, and Carey McWilliams, a rising young attorney, author of a biography of Ambrose Bierce and destined eventually to become editor of *The Nation*. I met the grizzled muckraker, Lincoln Steffens, and his passionate young wife, Ella Winter, who were intrigued by the thought of a book about a California poet having been written *in absentia*, as it were.

I caught the *Daylight* at Castroville Junction and was met in Glendale by Newell and Ritchie. We held a protracted, convivial reunion. Ritchie was getting established as a printer. Newell was unhappy in his marriage. Dr. Stelter had sent word for me to come and see him about a job. When I did my hopes were dashed. Not only had the trustees denied his request for an added position, they had cut the faculty salary scale. Thousands were out of work. I realized the extent of the Depression.

My brother George had married a wealthy Flintridge girl, Edwina Martin, and they and a newborn son were living in one of her family's houses on Prospect Boulevard in Pasadena. They generously urged me to stay with them. George had been hard hit by the Depression, and he was drinking too much. I helped hold the house together. I liked my sister-in-law, a canary bird of a girl, educated in Italy, and fond of music and art. A bond of affection was formed between Edwina, called Ted, and me; we became like brother and sister.

I felt well physically, drank little, and had stopped smoking. The endless novel had been scrapped and I had begun a shorter, tighter version. Phil Hanna paid me $50 for an article on Jeffers, based on my visit to Tor House. I felt rich, and proceeded to look up old girl friends and found new ones, some of whom I took to call on MacIntyre at his cabin. He had married again, a sturdy brunette, and one day in the dry autumn when I saw smoke from a forest fire in the direction of La Crescenta, I took my brother's Model-A Ford roadster and drove to the scene. There was Marian MacIntyre on the roof, fighting flying embers with a wet sack, and looking like one of the Furies in François Rude's frieze on the Arc de Triomphe. I seized a sack and joined her. Between us we saved the house by the time Mac arrived from UCLA. He was henceforth a little more willing to forgive me for having written on Jeffers, whose unrhymed verse he detested.

In the Depression I found myself like a powerful new engine, tooled and fueled, running idle with nowhere to go. I wanted work of usefulness and promise. There was none for a person of my background and training. Dance music? No. That way lay aesthetic and emotional bankruptcy.

Then, nearly three and a half years since we had parted in Paris, I met Fay again. She was married, with a five-month-old baby boy, named for her brother Norman. Her husband, an older man, was from a family of intellectuals. He too was out of work and had gone off somewhere, leaving Fay and the babe in a one-room Hollywood apartment. We met at the college sorority house. It was homecoming for us both. She was terribly thin, and more beautiful than ever.

After her divorce Fay and I were married in the Ventura County Court House by a Justice of the Peace on March 26, 1934, in the presence of George and Ted. We chose the place for sentimental reasons: both Clark and George had been married there.

Our gay wedding announcement printed by Ritchie brought word from Dr. Stelter that when Dean Cleland had seen the announcement he solemnly declared it to be another of Larry Powell's escapades, and that it wouldn't last six months. As I write this now, Fay is setting the tea table, in the thirty-third year of our marriage. Our son Norman, a UCLA graduate, too is happily married, to Armena Boyajian. He and his younger brother Wilkie grew up together in a happy boyhood. Fortune blessed us in their affectionate relationship, and in their love for us.

Fay and I honeymooned for three months in a furnished cottage in Three Arches, now called South Laguna. To pay the total rent of $45 and give us something for food, I sold my saxophones and clarinet, the final break with a past more cacophonous than mellifluous. We had our first car, a 1925 Star coupé, a wedding present from Uncle Harold. Aunt Emma had died and he was happily remarried to Aunt Jessie. They were living in Westwood near UCLA. It wasn't much of a car, having cost, he told me, only $25, but it held our clothes, Normie and his crib, and Black Bart, Newell's loan of a huge and gentle German Shepherd, sired by the movie dog Strongheart. We loaded up and away we went.

What was our plan? Free-lance writing. First, a book about D. H. Lawrence. Travel pieces. A bohemian life, working just enough to keep a roof over our heads and food in our stomachs. Fay did not want me to become an academic man. The Fishers were living nearby and we had some memorable meals together, while Al read aloud from the *Ghost*. Ritchie and Newell came down weekends. We made a congenial group and vaguely planned an artists' commune in Baja California, with assets and labor in common. We believed that destiny had brought us together for a cultural purpose and that somewhere in the Southwest we were meant to colonize as a creative group. Fisher was reading the Urquhart-Motteux Rabelais, and wrote bawdy ballads in which the group of us figured. Eventually, of the four, Ritchie and I alone made our careers in Los Angeles. Fisher moved for good to Smith College in Massachusetts and Newell became identified with Monterey County and the Big Sur.

Dr. Bieler also came to see us, grave and tender, and advised Fay wisely on her and the baby's regimen. I wrote stories, sketches, reviews, and received rejection slips for them all. My application for a Guggenheim Fellowship to write on D. H. Lawrence was not granted. Our money dwindled and no more was in prospect.

Then Ritchie, on an overnight visit, reported that Jake Zeitlin needed a secretary-stenographer. Ritchie knew of my Link-Belt experience ten years before and had mentioned my name to Jake. My Jeffers book was in press, due to appear in the summer of 1934, and Jake and I had met several times. I remembered him from the Vroman job of 1929, when I used to drive the store's truck to pick up special orders at Los Angeles bookstores. Jake's hole-in-the-wall shop at Sixth and Hope was stocked with English imports, prints and drawings by local artists. The customers were unusual. The shop was permeated with a rich fragrance I never could trace, though it might have come from the Turkish cigarettes Jake favored. Zeitlin was a fascinating character, the runaway poet son of an orthodox Fort Worth Russian Jew, whose first job in Los Angeles had been shovelling manure on the Doheny estate. He had entered the book-trade and, in spite of the Depression, prospered. Now he was planning a larger shop across Sixth Street between Hope and Grand. He was vital and magnetic.

That evening of Ritchie's visit a telegram was delivered by a bicyclist from the Laguna office of Western Union. It was from Jake Zeitlin and asked that I telephone him collect. I went to the nearest phone, then returned to report to Ritchie and Fay.

"Jake wants me to start next week on July 1."

"What will this do to your writing?" Fay asked.

"I told him half-time only. Mornings, nine to one, five days a week. I'll have afternoons and evenings to write."

"What will he pay?" Ritchie asked.

"Thirty dollars a month."

"Primavera Press will give you $7.50 a month to bill, wrap, and ship orders," Ritchie added.

"We can live on $37.50," Fay said.

And we did, thanks to her. We moved into a partly furnished house on Loma Vista Place in the Edendale section of Los Angeles, a five cent trolley car ride from Jake's shop. It was a house owned by the Bank of America, one of many they had taken over when the mortgage was defaulted. Our rent was $10 a month, including utilities.

I worked two-and-a-half years for Jake Zeitlin, and the experience was fully as educational and useful as the years at Occidental and Dijon. It proved a base on which my subsequent authority as a bookman was established. Jake proved to be more than an exotic character. I came to love him as a rare human being, in spirit, compassion, understanding, and creative imagination, truly one of the great bookmen of our times. He was also one of my best teachers. What I got from Jake was not money, although I earned more the longer I stayed with him. I received a varied experience in the antiquarian book-trade. I typed letters and copy for catalogs, dressed windows, wrapped and delivered packages, and came to know books, manuscripts, and prints at first hand. And I met the best people, not only of Los Angeles, but from near and far, the bookish people, rich and poor, powerful and humble, who were drawn to the shop. It was the cultural heart of the city. Lawyers, doctors, clergymen, educators, writers, actors, musicians, came and went, browsed and bought; and I knew them all.

There was Paul Jordan-Smith, literary editory of the Los Angeles *Times*, who came into the shop, always on fire about his latest literary discovery—*Anthony Adverse*, *Gone with the Wind*, *Tortilla Flat*, *The Daring Young Man on the Flying Trapeze*. As a result of Smith's holding forth, I personally collected the early books of Steinbeck and Saroyan. There was the Right Reverend William Bertrand Stevens, Episcopal Bishop of Los Angeles, who liked my book on Jeffers and invited me to eat with him in the Dairy Lunch across the street. There was Edward Weston, the photographer, and Millard Sheets, the painter, and Rockwell Kent whose woodcuts illustrated my Jeffers book. Weston was taken with Fay's beauty and asked her to sit for him. I shall forever regret our having had, for some unremembered reason, to break the date. And Elmer Belt, the surgeon, who, when I delivered books to his office across the street, had me bring them into the room where, figuratively, the poor patient lay etherized, while Dr. Belt pored over his purchases. It was then that the groundwork was laid which eventually brought Belt's monumental Vinciana collection to UCLA.

Jake's shop was a business, true, but it was also a constantly changing work of art, with books and people, dreams and ideas, in a brilliant kaleidoscope. Ritchie was in and out, as we published more books, and his press flourished. Newell had broken free and remarried and gone off to China for a year to study their ancient ways of working stone and bronze. The Primavera Press had added me to the directorate and raised my salary to $12.50 a month. Fay and I did the billing, wrapping and shipping at the Ritchie press once a week, at the same time joining Ward and his wife Janet in libation and collation. "Ritchie's Roadhouse," we called it.

Phil Hanna gave me an assignment which led to a long connection with *Westways*. Accustomed himself to writing the quarterly book reviews, he called on me once at the last minute to do it for him. I had only overnight to

49

read and review a dozen books. Fay read to me, as we worked all night. It netted us $35. Hanna liked what I did, and I have been doing it ever since, monthly since 1946; and by it I have earned a readership numbering in the thousands. Another assignment was to make a report on San Francisco's gourmet restaurants. With an advance of $50 we took off on a week's vacation in Newell's yellow Mercer, and relished memorable food and drink, particularly at Jack's on Sacramento Street. Coming home down the San Joaquin Valley, I raced another car, burned out a main bearing, limped into Merced and, having spent the $50, had to wire Ritchie to send $10 for repairs and an overnight hotel bill.

Fay helped in every way. Considering that she had never kept house or cooked or managed finances, she proved an able mistress of our modest home, now grown to four as Wilkie Haines Powell appeared on October 7, 1935. My mother had returned from Europe and 'lived near us in a little place of her own. The Depression began to lift a bit as government spending had effect.

The Depression had disillusioned me politically and I rejected the Republicanism of my father's time, and registered as a Communist, a gesture I was to pay for sixteen years later. We spent happy times at Capo di Monte, feasting there at Thanksgiving and Christmas. Dean Cleland was no longer my nemesis. President Bird was supreme at the college, and in 1935, thirty years after Jeffers' graduation, we arranged a campus exhibition of his work, with a catalog printed by Ritchie and the exhibition room graced with sculptures by Newell. We were slowly making our way as members of the cultural community.

Yet I was increasingly unhappy at Zeitlin's. More and more it became clear that his was a one-man business. Beyond a point Jake was unwilling, more than that, unable to delegate or to share. The most likely step for me to take was into a bookshop of my own. We discussed it with the Bells, and they were willing to advance some capital. I could not finally reconcile the idea with a need I felt to be socially useful, in some way that did not involve buying and selling, even though the trade was in intellectual and artistic merchandise. And so our life changed.

BACK TO SCHOOL

A chipmunk of a public librarian, Albert C. Read, head of the Order Department in the Los Angeles Public Library, was the man who diverted me into what became the mainstream of my life. Beginning in January 1936, Jake assigned me full time to outside selling, calling on collectors at their homes and offices, making the rounds of the movie studios and public and university libraries. I had the use of his car and larger book bag. I did not like the role of book peddler. At the MGM Studios in Culver City I was kept waiting for an hour by a script writer who had asked to see a first edition of *A Shropshire Lad*, priced at $200. When I was finally showed into his office, I found him in dressing robe and slippers, lying on a couch. He looked at the book, liked what he saw, then proposed to pay the price less the sales tax. I took the book from him, put it in my bag, and walked out. He followed me to the parking lot, and there we made the deal, on my terms, full price plus tax. Years later he proved a generous donor to the library I had come to head.

The motivating force behind my persistence and modest success as a salesman was the fact that I was no longer on salary, but on commission, whereby I received fifty per cent of the gross profits on each sale. This however led me to overprice everything.

Then one day in the Public Library, across the street from the shop, after I had finished showing some recent English typographical books to Albert Read, he took me in his office and said,

"You should be buying for, not selling to libraries."

"What do you mean?"

"You should follow my example and leave the book business for library work."

It seems that Read had been the manager of Fowler's, one of the city's oldest bookstores, then had taken courses at the public library and became their chief buyer.

He ushered me into the adjoining office of the city librarian, the vivacious ginger-haired Althea Hester Warren. He sat me beside her desk, left the room, and Miss Warren proceeded to seal my fate.

"Of course you should be a librarian," she said. "And with your doctor's degree, you belong in a university library, at UCLA or USC or one of the colleges. They need men like you."

"What do I have to do?"

"Go to school for a year and obtain a library credential."

"I don't want to go back to school and besides I can't afford to. I have a wife and two children and no money."

"Nonsense," she laughed. "When there's a will there's a way. And you must go to Berkeley. Dean Mitchell specializes in training young men like you."

She transferred her will to me, and I went home and told Fay of the idea.

She laughed. "You a librarian? You're too lively, and besides, you read books!"

We went to see Dr. Stelter. He was enthusiastic. He also converted Fay. So it was decided. I had everything but the money. We were unwilling to ask the Bells for help. And then, once again, fortune and friendship came into conjunction.

Through the bookshop I had come together again with Alonzo Beecher Cass, a South Pasadena school days friend, and the trap drummer in our high school dance orchestra, who had gone on to more serious things. While I was studying in France, he had been on the arduous road to an M.D. from Stanford, and was now a resident physician at the Hollywood Hospital. His hobby was painting water colors. He came from a wealthy family and had always lived a generous, open-handed life; his red hair, green eyes, and freckled skin compounding a natural charm.

We had become friends with him and his wife Libby and one evening, soon after my talk with Read and Miss Warren, the Casses came to dinner. Fay was fast becoming a good cook and had prepared a succulent meat loaf made of ground beef heart, which could then be bought for nine cents a pound. We had wine too, an ordinary red from a Cucamonga winery; and after dinner while Cass and I were in the kitchen washing up, I told him of my dream of becoming a librarian, a dream which seemed doomed because of our poverty.

"Will a thousand dollars help?" he asked.

"We could almost make it on that," I said, "plus what I might earn working part-time. But who's got that much money to spare?"

"I am coming into an inheritance in April when I am thirty. A thousand of it's yours, no strings, pay it back if and when you are able."

I was so excited I pitched a wine glass at the wall, and

the girls came rushing into the kitchen to find Cass and me toasting the future with a freshly poured round.

His money came on April 1, no fooling, and he wrote me a check for $1,000, then he and his wife took a vacation trip to Europe. The Ritchies and Powells and Zeitlins saw them off on the *Chief*. We were all tight, following a farewell luncheon, and I had a flask of whiskey on my hip. When Ritchie hoisted me up to kiss Libby Cass goodbye, as she leaned out of the Pullman's open window, the bottle was dislodged and fell with a crash on the platform. The whiskey flowed, the pungent fumes arose. We groaned at the tragedy. Dr. Cass leaned out the window, as the train began to move, and in a voice that could be heard all over the station, bellowed,

"Powell, stop wasting good whiskey!"

I took Cass at his word that there was no hurry to repay him. It was on April 1, 1965, no fooling, just thirty years after his loan, that I sent him a check for $1,000.

Our plans went forward. A personal interview being required, Dean Mitchell asked me to present myself to University Librarian John E. Goodwin at UCLA. They had been classmates at the Albany Library School and Mitchell played a leading role in building Goodwin's staff to strength. I wrote Goodwin and heard nothing. Two weeks went by. I queried Mitchell what to do. Write again, he replied. I did, this time a postcard. I received an appointment by return mail. Probably Mitchell had prodded Goodwin.

It was on April 16, 1936, that I first went to the cathedral-like UCLA Library. On my way to Goodwin's office, as hidden away as was his own nature, I stood in the octagonal rotunda, among students going their bookish ways, admired the pink tiles and creamy ceramic panels. It was then and there that I experienced a moment of truth, a sudden illumination, in which I knew that this was my destined place. That night in my journal, I wrote,

"The interview with Mr. Goodwin was brief. I found him a dignified, graying, essentially non-commital man. Yes, he said, there should be a future for you in academic library work. I did not ask nor did he say anything about an eventual job at UCLA, although I was certain that my future lay there, even as his successor."

Apparently Goodwin recommended me, for I was admitted to the graduate library school at Berkeley for the fall term which began in August, 1936. I was required to study German concurrently with the library course. German is a language which never appealed to me—and still doesn't, believing as I do that it was only through music that the Teutonic spirit purified itself. In order to get a head start, Fay and I enrolled in an evening high school German class.

We moved north in July, the four of us and belongings somehow loaded in an old Paige-Jewett sedan which, at $35, had upgraded the worn-out Star and an intermediate Willys-Knight. Her aunt gave Fay a small allowance, my Uncle Harold contributed to our rent in Berkeley, and I had lined up a part-time job, checking authors' references on the galley proofs of their books in process at the University Press. And we had the Cass thousand in the bank.

The Joads had nothing on us. We took two days to cover the 400 miles to Berkeley via the San Joaquin Valley. We slept the first night in a flea-ridden motel at Bakersfield. So eager were we to be on the road that we went off the next morning without baby Wilkie's tin pottie. The heat was fierce. The car overheated, making progress slow. Late in the afternoon at Tracy I foolishly bought a pint of grape brandy, and by the time we reached the apartment at 2726 Derby Street, off College Avenue in Berkeley, I was exhausted and a bit drunk. I couldn't find the key to the apartment. A peach tree in the front yard had dropped its ripe fruit and I slipped and fell in the squishy mass. I couldn't force a window. In despair we drove to my cousin Carolyn's and her husband Grenville returned with us and managed to get a window open. It was a nightmare. Only the baby boys enjoyed it, especially the gooey peaches.

That wasn't the worst thing that happened. In July, a week before classes were to start, I drove to Los Gatos to meet John Steinbeck. I had collected his early books in every edition and issue and he agreed to autograph them for me. We had been in correspondence. He was nearing the end of his heroic labor in writing *The Grapes of Wrath*, and a series of postcards, written in his spidery hand that could get a thousand words on a card, reported on the progress of his manuscript and his corresponding bad health. We spent the day talking and drinking wine. By evening, when it was time to drive back to Berkeley, I was drunk. Steinbeck and his wife Carol tried to persuade me to spend the night, but as neither they nor we in Berkeley had a phone, I did not want to worry Fay by my failure to return, and so I set out.

The next thing I knew, several hours later and sober, I was being booked in the Santa Clara County Jail in San Jose. I demanded to know why I was there. The desk sergeant laughed. "You're lucky to be alive."

"What do you mean?"

"I mean you wrapped your car around a telephone pole and there's not a scratch on you."

"Let me go," I said. "My wife will be worried."

He laughed and locked me up in the drunk tank. The bunks were full. I took my coat off, made a pillow for my head, and slept on the floor. I have always been able to sleep, no matter the place or time.

In the morning I was allowed to telephone to my

cousin. I asked her and Grenville to pick up Fay and come and bail me out. They did. We drove by the wrecking yard and looked at the car. "Wrapped around" was the correct phrase. It was a total loss.

Not only did I come out of it with a whole skin; all of Steinbeck's books survived. The police car that took me to the jail must have been manned by a natural-born collector. He gathered up the dozen precious volumes and they were returned to me in the morning. Five years later, in need of money and no longer interested in the post-*Grapes* Steinbeck, I sold my collection to Harvard, and it is now in the Houghton Library. *Habent sua fata libelli*, including a one-night sojourn in the Santa Clara County Jail.

That was one of the cruellest things I did to Fay, who had 'spent a sleepless night waiting for me to come home. It should have persuaded me to give up drinking. My ability was fast diminishing to consume any alcohol without experiencing intoxication. It was another two years, however, before I went on the wagon for good.

I had mixed feelings about the year in library school. Dean Sydney B. Mitchell was on sabbatical leave, and I did not meet him until the year was nearly over. The women instructors were not inspiring, although Edith M. Coulter's reference lectures were marked by dry humor. The most human person was Katherine C. Anderson, a Portland, Oregon librarian, who was filling in for Mitchell. She taught the course in book selection, using as text Helen E. Haines' newly published *Living with Books*, one of the few humanistic works in library literature. She made allowances for my unorthodox preparation for library school. We became friends in after years.

The Book Arts course was given by Acting Dean Della J. Sisler, who also taught cataloging by rule of thumb. We had incompatible tastes in typography.

When I proposed to arrange an exhibit and read a paper on the work of Ward Ritchie, Miss Sisler declared categorically that there was no fine printing being done in Los Angeles. I went ahead anyway and displayed the work Ritchie sent up on loan. Miss Sisler grudgingly admitted its excellence.

In the spring I arranged a Jeffers exhibition in the university library, the first ever held there of the poet's work. Robin and Una drove up from Carmel to see it and came to our flat for tea. Fay was touched by Robin's grave courtesy.

It was a bad year for her, the coldest in many winters, the flat was unheated, our money limited. We had no car, and I was away on campus or studying most of the time. In addition to the library curriculum, I was also taking first-year German, auditing an advanced course in bibliography, and working for the University Press. The director of the Press, Samuel T. Farquhar, liked to take me drinking when he could persuade me to play the piano in bars. He was another of the influential people I had met at Jake's shop. My old trap drummer friend, Clinton Williams, was taking his Ph.D. in English, and he and his wife used our garage for their Model-A Ford and allowed us to use the car occasionally. Soon after the great Oakland Bay Bridge was opened, Fay and I and the children drove over and back in the long parade of cars. I was writing book reviews for a weekly called *Los Angeles Saturday Night*, and one of the first was of C. F. MacIntyre's *Poems*, published by Macmillan.

A month before graduation, I wrote to Goodwin, to apply for a job at UCLA. I never received an answer. I also wrote to USC and to several movie studio research libraries. Nothing came of any of these applications, most of which went unanswered. The library school itself made no effort to place me. Miss Sisler barely gave me a passing grade. Miss Coulter was pleasant enough, but she was opposed on principle to men in library work. She was also a Bay Region chauvinist, and suffered from regional myopia. The very thought of Los Angeles and UCLA displeased her. These prejudices increased as she aged.

What made the year bearable was the university library itself, its deep and lofty stacks, and the Bancroft Library, housing a million and more volumes. Every free moment I spent there, browsing and reading. Once I was up on the highest stack level, poring through the Transactions of the Académie de Dijon, nostalgic for the golden years in Burgundy, when the University Librarian, Harold L. Leupp, a martinet, came along. He rarely deigned to recognize a mere library school student, but this time he paused to chat. I had no intention of applying to him for a position. The Berkeley library atmosphere was, and is to this day, as cold as the granite building that houses it.

Through an introduction from Jake Zeitlin, I called on the legendary Herbert E. Bolton, historian and director of the Bancroft Library, a great scholar and trainer of scholars. A marathon monologist, he was talking when I entered his office; he kept talking, and was still talking when I left, so I can hardly report our conversation.

Clinton Williams urged me to audit Professor T. K. Whipple's seminar in American Literature, reporting that Whipple had praised my book on Jeffers. I walked in unannounced one day on the seminar which was held on the floor above the library school, Whipple stopped lecturing. There was a dead silence.

"May I ask who you are?" he demanded.

"Only a library school student," I confessed.

The students laughed, and Whipple resumed his remarks. I learned later that the *San Francisco Examiner* had been planting reporters in Berkeley classes, seeking evidence of a Red Plot being fomented on campus, and Whipple had taken me for such.

I made only one friend among the fifty students in my class, the girl who by reason of alphabetical arrangement sat at the desk in front of me, Fay Allene Porter, of Reedley in the San Joaquin Valley. She alone expressed interest in the Jeffers exhibit. She asked if I would read some poems by a Valley friend of hers. "If they're typed," was my reply. That is how I came to know the work of William Everson, and eventually the man himself, destined as Brother Antoninus to be one of the original poets of our time.

Dean Mitchell returned a few weeks before graduation and he and his wife Rose were friendly to Fay and me. He was a native of Montreal and spoke fluent French. It was a friendship that grew warmer eventually and endured until the Mitchells died. The only job prospect he could see for me was an internship at the Stephens College Library, Columbia, Missouri, that paid $2,400 a year. Fay and I dreamed of such a salary as being the answer to all our needs. We never attained it. My first position, later, at the Los Angeles Public Library was at $1,500. I began at UCLA at $1,620 and rose in five years to $1,860. Then as head librarian, I jumped to $5,000. So we never were to receive our dream salary of $2,400.

The Stephens job went to someone else. Years later, sitting on a special faculty appointment committee at UCLA, I was called upon to cast the deciding vote on the man who had not appointed me at Stephens. Yes, I voted yes.

REACHING FOR THE LOWEST RUNG

The time came to leave
Berkeley. I had earned another degree, and still there
was no job nor any prospect of one. Newell moved us
south in his Dodge pickup truck. Fay, Norman, and
Wilkie rode with him in the cab, I in the open back in a
crevice between our worldly goods. It was a long, cold,
inauspicious ride back down the Valley, but we were
given a warm welcome by George and Ted, now living
on an isolated ranch in Altadena at the foot of the Sierra
Madre. We stayed there a few weeks and then Uncle
Harold and Aunt Jessie offered us their spacious Westwood house while they were on a trip to the eastern
United States.

And Jake Zeitlin came through with a special assignment. He had D. H. Lawrence's manuscripts on consign-
ment from Frieda, and wanted a sales catalog of them.
I was the one to compile it, having assembled a collection
of Lawrence's works and the books about him. The
manuscripts were in the California Bank at Sixth and
Grand, a block from the shop, but Frieda would not
allow them to be removed. I worked every day in the

steel vault, studying the diversity of manuscripts and making notes.

Then in the evening, home in Westwood, I pored through my books in search of descriptive notes to accompany the bibliographical descriptions. For a month's work Jake paid me $100. The catalog was printed by Ward Ritchie, with a Foreword by Aldous Huxley, and bore the imprint of the Los Angeles Public Library.

This is how that unlikely association happened. My window-dressing experience at Zeitlin's shop led to my making library displays of books, as I did twice during the school year at Berkeley. Now the Lawrence manuscripts had come to us directly from Harvard where they had been on exhibit in the Widener Library.

One day on my lunch hour, I went to see Miss Warren for the first time since a year before, when she had changed my life.

"How would you like to have an exhibit of D. H. Lawrence's manuscripts?" I asked her.

"Love it," was her characteristically enthusiastic reply.

That's all it took. And that is why Althea Warren was one of the best librarians of her time. Her responses were immediate and affirmative. She was in the great yea-saying tradition.

I arranged a show of the manuscripts, supplemented by my own collection of books and crowned by Knud Merrild's oil portrait of Lawrence borrowed from its owner, Walter C. Arensberg, another of my bookshop friends. Jake induced Aldous Huxley to open the exhibition with a talk on Lawrence. It was a triumph. Hundreds were turned away. Miss Warren beamed.

The catalog was paid for by Dr. Elmer Belt, one more of the many generous things he and his wife Ruth did for Jake and Ward and me down through the years. Although I erred in ascribing one early manuscript to Lawrence, when it was actually in the hand of the "Miriam" of *Sons and Lovers,* the catalog drew a warm notice in the *New York Times Book Review.*

The $100 from Jake went for food and bus fare. My uncle and aunt came home and we moved to a cottage in Eagle Rock, not far from the college and a ten cent streetcar ride downtown. I don't know how we paid the rent. We were very poor and reluctant to ask our relatives for help. After all, I had three academic degrees, which, surely should have been worth something in the market place. They weren't. There was still widespread unemployment and uncertainty. Most libraries where I applied for a job regarded me as overqualified. I suppose I was, but I could also work a nail-puller, wrap a package, dress an exhibit, and I was an expert typist.

I went to see Miss Warren. "You got me into this, now get me out!" She beamed. "You don't belong in a public library, as I told you from the beginning, and besides our civil service exam is not given again until next February, but I will put you on the temporary substitute list."

And she did, at $125 a month, and I worked in a variety of jobs for the next six months, in the Teacher's Room of the main library, on the desk in the branch library across from USC, and finally in the Order Department under Mr. Read. It was good experience, but it was temporary and occasional, substituting only when regular staff was ill or on vacation. I also arranged two more exhibits in the main library's cental showcases, one of my John Steinbeck collection—publication of *Of Mice and Men* had brought him his first popular success —and of Printers of Los Angeles. When I proposed to Ritchie that I repeat my Berkeley exhibit of his work, he suggested that I enlarge it to recognize his fellow printers, past and present; and so, for the first time, a comprehensive showing was made of local fine printing.

One day Miss Warren summoned me to report Scripps College's search for a head librarian and that she had recommended me to the president. The job paid $2,400. There followed my first experience with the shilly-shallying that characterizes many academic people —cautious, uncertain, and indecisive. I was interviewed by president, dean, chairman of library committee, by everyone but janitor and gardener, and then after being kept in suspense for two months, the job went to a high school librarian, Dorothy M. Drake. She is still there, one of the best college librarians, and my colleague and friend.

How I wanted that job, both for the $2,400 and for the responsibility and challenge it presented, and how grateful I am that I didn't get it.

In order to earn money I got the word around that I was available, at $1.00 an hour, to do private library cataloging. My one and only job was to buy and arrange books for a library room in a newly built mansion in Bel Air. I bought them wholesale by size and color and shelved them in harmony with the room's decor. I thus earned ten or fifteen dollars, and the gratitude of those local booksellers whose shelves I cleared of many a linear foot of complete works.

Then, in January 1937, Dean Mitchell wrote that there would be a beginning job at UCLA as of the first of February and for me to remind John Goodwin of my availability. It was a lowly job, Mitchell warned me, consisting of routine accessioning, and that I was over-qualified and would doubtless be unhappy in it. He nevertheless wanted, I learned later, to keep pressure on Goodwin to add more men to his staff, which then consisted of three men and thirty-two women. More men were coming to library school and Mitchell wanted to ensure their placement in the profession.

This time I didn't write. I presented myself at Goodwin's office and he received me kindly. Without any words—he was one of the most silent men I have ever known—he beckoned me to follow him and led me through what seemed a maze of halls and stairs and rooms, until we had reached a large stack room in the lower depths. Still no word from him. I looked at the shelves. Californiana, thousands of volumes and pamphlets, a glorious sight. I looked at Goodwin. There was a faint smile on his face.

"Well?" he finally said. "Can you accession this collection?"

"When do I start?" was my reply.

"February first."

"Agreed," I said.

It was the Robert Ernest Cowan collection, a massive library formed by the bibliographer of California history and former bookseller and librarian to William Andrews Clark, Jr. The university had bought it in 1936 for $50,000 and stored it, hoping someone on the staff would have some knowledge of the subject. My predecessor at UCLA, John J. Lund, whose resignation to take a better job at Duke University led to my appointment, held a Ph.D. in Germanic linguistics, not the best preparation for accessioning the Cowan collection.

Goodwin had observed on my application that I had reviewed Californiana for *Westways*, written a book on Jeffers, and had worked for Zeitlin, one of whose specialties was Californiana. I had come to know Cowan himself, a frequent visitor to the shop and who, since leaving Clark's employ, had again become a bookseller.

CLIMBING THE UCLA LADDER

On the first day of February 1938, I began a career at UCLA which was to keep me there twenty-eight and a half years, during which I saw the University Library's stock of 285,000 volumes increased by 2,000,000, the Clark Memorial Library transformed from a bookish mausoleum to a center of biblioscholarly activity, a staff of 35 grow to 300, a library school come into being, and UCLA become known internationally as a dynamic place of books and learning. During all of those years, even the first half dozen, when I seemed to be getting nowhere, I never wavered in my conviction that *this was the place*. Fortune and friendship brought me there at the precise time a librarian of my temperament was needed. If it was made for me, I was made for it.

On my first day at work, Goodwin led me back to Room 34. There I was given a table and chair, a typewriter, and strips of accession cards, and I set to work listing the Cowan collection. It took months, during which I never saw Goodwin again. My immediate supervisor was a young woman librarian, formally polite, who gave me a minimum of instructions on procedure. It was an ideal assignment. The salary of $1,620 represented a $10 a month increase over what I had earned at the Public Library. We moved to Sherman Oaks, a short run through Beverly Glen from the San Fernando Valley to campus. We bought a Studebaker sedan called a Rockne.

And again I experienced the joy of immediate access to a scholarly collection of world literature. Though smaller than Berkeley's, the UCLA collection was choice. Goodwin and staff, with faculty advice, had laid strong foundations for the great library UCLA was destined to become. I took home load after load of books in a dozen fields—American and French literature, bibliography, travel—and went on a reading spree. My supervisor encouraged me to recommend library purchases, and I concentrated on neglected areas, such as bibliography, typography, and books about books and writing, and also I began to fill gaps in French literature. Stendhal and Baudelaire, for example, were hardly represented in the collection. The Germanic section was without the works of Rilke. The collection lacked Joyce's *Ulysses*, most of Lawrence and Hemingway. During the next five years thousands of volumes were acquired on my recommendation. I also persuaded my department head to place a standing order for the publications of James Laughlin's *New Directions;* and later that tall, sandalled, imaginative friend of literature came to thank me, saying UCLA was the first library to show unlimited confidence in his taste.

My work with the Cowan materials was like a private seminar in Californian history, leading me to friendship with John Walton Caughey, professor of Western history at UCLA, and with his chief assistant, graduate student William B. Rice, a brilliantly promising researcher and writer who died in 1942 while climbing the Grand Teton.

It led me also to Cowan himself, the elegant old Irish bookman, living in retirement in the house near the Clark Library. My supervisor encouraged me every few weeks to gather "snags" in the Cowan collection and take them to "Sir Robert" for enlightenment. Those were memorable visits to the old gentleman who received me in his upper floor study, smoking the fine Havanas he favored (their fragrance evoked memories of my father), commenting on the provenance and significance of the books and pamphlets as I produced them from my bag. I had become another kind of peddler than the one I'd been at Zeitlin's shop.

In the course of accessioning the Cowan collection, using his own inventory as a guide to the items on the shelf, I found myself unable one day to locate one of the collection's rarest items, the first printing, 1849, of the *Constitution of California,* a mere pamphlet valued nevertheless at $1,000. My search led upstairs to a WPA book mending project, staffed by a couple of women whose job was to repair torn bindings and make cardboard covers for pamphlets. I arrived as one of them was about to staple the *Constitution* into a binder. I snatched it from her and took it to my supervisor. She was mildly amused by my indignation and passed me on to Goodwin. He listened while I explained what happened to pamphlets that had been stapled. Rust set in, spread, and eventually ate away the surrounding paper. This in itself did not impress him. Only when I went back downstairs and brought up the inventory and showed him the $1,000 evaluation, did he ask,

"What do you propose we do?"

"Instruct the women to make cloth-covered board cases for all such valuable pamphlets and then place them in the rare book room."

I knew of course that there was no rare book room. There was in the stacks only a locked cage wherein a miscellaneous jumble of items was segregated, with no one particular in charge.

Now it happened that Goodwin never failed to be interested when a craft matter presented itself. He was an expert cabinet worker. Once when I discovered that the library lacked the monumental biographies of Hearst's mother and father, commissioned of John Henry Nash, I mentioned it to Goodwin and asked if he would request copies of the newspaper publisher. He thought it useless. I wrote to Hearst at San Simeon, asking for the books on behalf of UCLA. Copies came within a week, gorgeous volumes in full vellum bindings. I proudly took them in to Goodwin. His sheepish look warmed as he drew the books from their fleece bags and noticed that the covers were warping. "I can fix that," he said. And he did, using materials in the library basement to make wooden presses to hold the bindings flat.

Now he and I went back to the WPA women and Goodwin worked out with them the fabrication of folding cases. He allowed me henceforth to indicate what pamphlets were to be given this protection.

That was the beginning of what eventually became the Department of Special Collections. Alas, even that early start was too late. Scores of rare and valuable Cowan pamphlets had been stapled into binders and placed on the open stack shelves. Hundreds of rare bound volumes had had their title pages perforated, their end papers and top and bottom edges ink stamped.

The entire system was at fault. I set about correcting it to the best of my then limited authority.

An invitation to present a paper at a regional conference of college and university librarians was my opportunity to prepare "The Problem of Rare Books in the College and University Library"; and to gather material,

I sent a questionnaire to several academic libraries. One was the William L. Clements Library at the University of Michigan, whose Director, Randolph G. Adams, an historian turned librarian, had written an already classic essay in *The Library Quarterly* called "Librarians as Enemies of Books," and was engaged in a running skirmish with the ALA's hierarchy.

Adams did not answer my letter by letter. He came in person, arriving one day in the company of Jake Zeitlin. They swept me along with them to Goodwin's office.

"I'm Randolph Adams," RGA said, "and I want you to give Powell a free hand with your rare books." Although Goodwin was somewhat stunned by this blunt approach, he also respected faculty authority, even when it was exercised by a Michigander, and he did what Randolph Adams suggested.

Henceforth Adams was my friend and champion. Again in 1939, at the ALA Conference in San Francisco, I presented a paper entitled "The Functions of Rare Books," in which I developed my ideas for their collection, care, and use in academic libraries.

The result of these two papers was to lead Dean Mitchell to think of me as a rare books librarian and nothing more, and when I replied, when we met at the conference, that I was interested in heading a college or university library, he said he would be unable to recommend me for such a position. If I had expressed to him my growing certainty that I was destined to succeed John Goodwin, he would have been scornful. I kept this certainty concealed.

My colleagues were puzzled when I kept turning down job offers from elsewhere: Knox College in Illinois, Macalester College in Minnesota, the Beverly Hills Public Library, Occidental College, MGM Studios Research Library.

When I reported these opportunities to Goodwin, he

encouraged me to stay at UCLA, saying that when the time came for him to retire—it was not far off—I would certainly be a strong candidate for the position. Yet when I said that I needed administrative experience and would he make me his assistant librarian, he would give no direct answer.

The other men librarians who had been on the staff when I came in 1938 had by 1942 all left, for one reason or another. A main one was the hostility toward men expressed by the older women on the staff and Goodwin's apparent domination by these women.

Seymour Lubetzky, the chief classifier, left when he was refused the salary that had gone to his predecessor in the position. Jens Nyholm, the head cataloger, had gone to Berkeley as assistant librarian to Mr. Leupp, and had sought to persuade me to accompany him as head of the order department. Remembering martinet Leupp, I declined, but suggested that Nyholm offer the position to Frank Lundy, chief cataloger at the Clark Library.

So this left Goodwin and me.

When time passed and I received no promotion, nor any encouragement from Goodwin, I recalled our conversation of two years before and that if he continued to keep me at the bottom, I would be in a poor position to succeed him. His reply was,

"The women won't stand for my promoting you over them."

I was angry. Goodwin gazed out the window.

"I feel that I should present my case to President Sproul," I said.

His reply was a pained smile.

I obtained an appointment with the big-voiced, dynamic head of the University of California and told my tale of woe.

"Stay around," he said. "I can't promise you anything, but I have heard good things about your work."

"Will I be a candidate to succeed Mr. Goodwin?"

"You will."

"I should be gaining experience now as assistant librarian."

"That's between you and him."

No more could I get out of that shrewd administrator. Nevertheless I was encouraged. I did not see Goodwin again. In fact I had no contacts with him, although I worked for him another year or more. One of our incompatibilities was his conservatism and my liberalism of social philosophy. Two incidents will illustrate this. A group of graduate students in political science came to me, as the only young man on the staff, to say that the faculty in their department refused to recommend that the library subscribe to the *Western Worker*, the Communist Party newspaper published in San Francisco. I advised them to present a petition to Goodwin. Soon thereafter I was summoned by Goodwin. He was angry.

"Did you put them up to this?" he demanded, showing me the students' petition.

I admitted that I had, at the same time calling his attention to the fact that the library was receiving from the German consul a gift subscription to the *Volkischer Beobachter*, the official Nazi newspaper and that it was being placed "on the stick" in the reading room.

"Dean Mitchell said that a library should balance its publications so that both sides should be represented. I believe the *Volkischer Beobachter* should be balanced by the *Western Worker*."

Then I waited for the axe to fall. It didn't. Goodwin agreed with me. Henceforth the *Western Worker* went "on the stick." He and I could have made a balanced team.

The other incident happened at the time of Upton Sinclair's sixtieth birthday, when I proposed a loan exhibit of Dr. Elmer Belt's large collection of Sinclair's books, in English and other languages. Goodwin said he would ask faculty advice as to the wisdom of publicizing the radical writer. The answer was no. The collection would have come to UCLA as a gift. Instead it was given to my Alma Mater, Occidental College, and so I could say that I batted .500 on that one.

The good things President Sproul had heard about me came from my friends on the faculty, and the way they came to be my friends was thus:

The first was C. F. MacIntyre, but unfortunately he left UCLA six months after I arrived. At the same time a transfer to Berkeley was arranged for him, he received a Guggenheim Fellowship for poetry and went off to Europe for a year. I wrote "Portrait of a Guggenheim Fellow" and sent it off unsuccessfully to *Saturday Review of Literature, Atlantic Monthly, Harper's, Virginia Quarterly Review.* It was eventually published in the *Wilson Library Bulletin,* which had published my first essays on books, their collecting and reading.

Soon after I joined the UCLA staff, Goodwin asked me to arrange library exhibits, as I had done at the Public Library. It seemed that no one on the staff wanted the assignment and the cases were standing empty. The only hitch was that my supervisor refused to grant me library time to arrange the exhibits, and so I had to collect the materials, annotate, and put them in after hours.

One Saturday afternoon I was down on my knees in back of one of the cases in the rotunda, when I saw a face peering at me through the glass. I stood up and so did the curious one. It was a faculty member, a handsome, gray-haired professor with a Southern accent.

"What *are* you up to?" he asked, looking at the materials on my book truck.

"I'm putting in a loan of Dr. Elmer Belt's Leonardo da Vinci collection. This portfolio is the *Codice Atlantico* facsimile."

The professor laughed and rubbed his front.

"Dr. Belt removed my kidney stones and did a damned good job of it."

I explained that in view of the library's lack of choice materials for exhibit, I planned a series of neighboring collectors' shows, starting with Dr. Belt, then Jean Hersholt's Hans Christian Andersen collection, Walter C. Arensberg's Bacon, and so on; and that I hoped thereby to form the nucleus for a Friends of the Library.

The professor listened, asked questions, then went on upstairs to his office. I learned later that he was Dr. Joseph B. Lockey, the Pan American historian, and more important, the chairman of the Faculty Research Committee, one of the most influential positions on campus. I had unknowingly made a key friend. Dr. Lockey was a member of a group of faculty bachelors who dined together once a week. The group included Waldemar Westergaard, Francis Crowley, Majl Ewing, Frederick Carey, and Edward N. Hooker. He told them of my work. They became interested in me. Other "young Turks" who reached a hand to me were Hugh G. Dick, Wayland D. Hand, Clinton N. Howard, Claude E. Jones, and Charles L. Mowat. Another senior history professor, Frank J. Klingberg, asked me to speak on library resources annually to his seminar.

During the five years of my responsibility, I arranged fifty displays, drawing on loan and library sources. One of the best was upon the occasion of Archibald MacLeish's giving the Charter Day address. It was called "Three Poets: Rilke, Yeats, MacLeish." MacLeish came to the rotunda to view it, the reason being that he knew that I had been one of the few librarians to speak out in favor of his appointment as Librarian of Congress. Jens Nyholm, Randolph Adams, and I, along with a few others, had sent a telegram to the poet at the time the

ALA was blasting FDR's appointment of MacLeish to the country's highest library post.

Goodwin must have been astonished when MacLeish asked to be taken to the library and when he thanked me for the exhibit, saying "You do me great honor to place my books with Yeats and Rilke."

Another exhibition I dressed was of the paintings of Dillwyn Parrish, M. F. K. Fisher's second husband. Parrish had been a writer most of his life, after attending Harvard as a classmate of E. E. Cummings, but also as an illustrator he had decorated books by his sister Anne. When as a sufferer from Buerger's disease he had a leg amputated and was told that his other leg and arms would follow and that he would die as a "basket case," he began to paint in oil in a race against death. There ensued a fantastic series of bold, beautiful paintings of flowers, fruits, vegetables, angels, and portraits of M. F. and himself.

I arranged with the Art Department on campus for an exhibition of Parrish's work to be held in the gallery on the top floor of the building. There was no elevator, and so M. F., Fay, and I lugged the paintings up and Parrish supervised their hanging, moving around the gallery on one leg and crutches, his face a mask of pain and joy.

He died soon after. I don't know where the paintings are today, other than ones owned by M. F. Many belonged to Anne Parrish who followed her brother in death. Fay and I have one, of kitchen utensils on a checked blue and white cloth.

Several pieces of research and writing that I carried out while a junior librarian, all done on my own time after hours, also played a key role in my advancement. They came out of my daily work. The first was a paper on John Fiske, the American historian, whose 12,000 volume library had been acquired by UCLA in 1925. I made a study of Fiske as a bookman and librarian—he

had been Justin Winsor's assistant librarian at Harvard—
and was invited to read the paper at a meeting of the
Bibliographical Society of America to be held at Cambridge in June 1941 in connection with the ALA Conference at Boston.

I had no money for the trip and asked Goodwin if the
library would send me as its delegate. He refused, although no one else from the staff was going to the
conference. When I asked if he thought the Faculty
Research Committee would give me a travel grant, he
said categorically that it would not, inasmuch as I, a
junior librarian, did not have faculty ranking. The University Librarian was the only member of the staff who
did.

At the end of the day I went upstairs to see Professor
Lockey. "Technically you don't qualify," he said, "but
put your request in a letter to me and let's see what can
be done."

I applied and was granted $125 for travel expenses. I
heard by the grapevine that Goodwin had urged the
Research Committee not to grant it, as a bad precedent.
This did nothing to improve our relationship.

Fay and I left our sons with their grandmothers and
drove to Boston. Goodwin relented and gave me travel
time, in addition to my month-long annual vacation. He
also named me to represent the library at the meeting of
the Association of Research Libraries, held in conjunction with the ALA and the BSA. In Cambridge we were
house guests of William A. Jackson, Librarian of the
Houghton Library, and in charge of the BSA meetings
in the Widener Library. This was the Bill Jackson I had
gone to high school with, but had never known well
because he was the "brain" of the class, already a brilliant student and destined to be the greatest rare book
librarian of our time.

The way we had come back together, after nearly

twenty years, was thus: I had read an article in *The Colophon* by Boise Penrose about a bibliographical tour of private English libraries taken by him and William A. Jackson. I wrote to Jackson at Harvard, asking "Are you the Bill Jackson of SPHS?" His affirmative reply invited me to contribute essays to *The Colophon*. I did, one on my Steinbeck collection, one on the books about D. H. Lawrence; and this in turn led to Jackson's inviting me to prepare the Fiske paper and for Fay and me to stay with him and his wife Dolly when we came to Cambridge.

Here again it was fortune and friendship in conjunction, for the events that led to my succeeding Goodwin were put in motion by Jackson.

I had prepared the Fiske paper with care and it required a full hour to read. At dinner the night before, Jackson informed me that each of the three papers on the morning's program would be limited to twenty minutes. I protested, to no avail. After dinner I withdrew to our room and proceeded to cut my pride and joy by two-thirds. It was a lesson I never forgot.

My paper was delivered to an audience of blue ribbon bibliographers that included Lawrence C. Wroth, George Parker Winship, T. Franklin Currier, H. M. Lydenberg, Thomas W. Streeter, and Randolph G. Adams. Afterward Lydenberg, the director of the New York Public Library, said that it was the most interesting paper he had ever heard read at a meeting of the BSA. It was printed in full in the *Papers* and Lockey circulated it widely on campus.

Next I proposed to the Editor of the *Pacific Historical Review* a paper on "Resources of Western Libraries for Research in History." This involved correspondence with and visits to a hundred or more institutions from Denver to the Pacific.

I had good fortune at the University Press with a monograph on Charles Edward Pickett, a reforming pamphleteer whose works I had discovered in the Cowan collection. I went ahead in free time and on my vacation in 1939, reading and collecting and writing, and completed *Philosopher Pickett*. When I showed the manuscript to Professor Majl Ewing and told him that I preferred not to submit it to a University Press committee, he persuaded me to reverse my stand, saying that their imprint on what was a piece of orthodox historical research would enhance my status on campus. He was right. The book passed committee reading and was published by the University Press in 1942.

After coming to work at UCLA, I spent many evenings in typing out Alfred Young Fisher's Dijon epic, *The Ghost in the Underblows*, then persuaded Ritchie to print it, providing I could raise $1,000 in advance subscriptions. Testimonials were solicited from Robinson Jeffers, William Everson, and other poets. A prospectus was mailed out, and brought in $500. The final $500 was advanced by Dr. Elmer Belt and the book appeared in 1940 in an edition of 300 copies with typographic decorations by Alvin Lustig. Except for a favorable notice by R. P. Blackmur in the *Southern Review*, the *Ghost* received no critical attention. It is ironical that the book is now esteemed as a typographical landmark. I still believe the poem to have elements of nobility, and certainly a hypnotic quality when read aloud.

Fisher and M. F. were divorced, and he joined the English department at Smith College and has taught there ever since. His vision faded with the *Ghost*, and never again did he write poetry.

Another beautiful book of poetry which I arranged for Ritchie to print and to which I also contributed a foreword was William Everson's *San Joaquin*. These were poems written under the influence of Jeffers, in the years before the poet's conversion to Roman Catholicism and his becoming the lay Brother Antoninus.

My foreword concluded, "If William Everson can work beyond the influences that keep his style from having complete originality, and if he can continue to extend his intellectual boundaries, he will take place along with his seaward neighbor as one of the few genuine poets California has produced." This came to pass.

I had a part-time student assistant named Steel Robson to help unpack incoming shipments and arrange the books on trucks—work that I had done as Vroman's shipping clerk. He was a big, rangy lad, a discus thrower on the track team, and he worked in silence. One day he came to me, holding the latest issue of the *Wilson Library Bulletin,* containing my essay called "Travel Notes from the Shipping Room."

"Shake," he said, holding out his hand. "I didn't know you were a librarian who read books."

Thus began a friendship that lasted until, as an ensign on board a destroyer, Steel Robson met a hero's death in the Battle of Leyte Gulf. In response to my request, his mother gave the library her son's books and established a poetry fund in his memory.

Those six years, 1938–1944, were the crucial years of my career. In spite of a lowly professional position, I established my reputation as bookman if not administrator. Goodwin's failure to involve me in the administration of the library, which I resented so at the time, was actually his greatest gift to me, for it left me free to think and dream and plan, untaxed by my routine tasks. Evenings, weekends, vacations were my own, and I used them mostly for the research and writing which carried my name to the faculty and beyond. Never again, until now in retirement, was I free of round-the-clock demands on my time and strength.

On September 4, 1940, I wrote in my journal, "I work continually, piecing together the daily tiles which will form the mosaic of my future. I want responsibility, and the opportunity to build and work with people and ideas and books. Given the chance, I can do work of lasting value."

TO THE TOP

Bill Jackson's motive in inviting me to Cambridge was not altogether bibliographical or social. He wanted his chief, Keyes D. Metcalf, to meet me with a view to my coming to the Harvard Library as head of the order department. I was flattered, of course, but my head was not turned. When Metcalf asked (through Jackson) what salary I would expect, my answer was, "Five thousand plus moving expenses." I was then at $1, 740 a year and, although I did not know it at the time, Goodwin's salary was only $5,000. Metcalf hoped to meet my figure and would let me know. He did, by the end of the year, again through Jackson, but not favorably. Pearl Harbor had happened.

I was not disappointed. I did not warm to Keyes Metcalf, believing him to be an administrator, rather than a bookman, although I did concede his genius in having brought Jackson to Harvard and given him a free hand. It was not until near the end of my career that I came to appreciate another aspect of the Metcalf genius, as an expert on library architecture. Then, when our new research library seemed doomed never to be funded by the legislature, I appealed to Keyes Metcalf to come as a consultant. He did and the building was funded. No one else could have done what he did. My biased view of him was corrected. Still I am glad I never went to Harvard, or to Berkeley, or to the Huntington Library where Mitchell at first thought I belonged. The only library in the land where I truly belonged was UCLA.

My rise there was extraordinary, from bottom to top rung in one move. Men inexperienced in administrative work, such as professors, have been placed in top library positions, but I know of no instance when a junior staff member, completely lacking in administrative experience, has been thus advanced. How did it happen? Again it was a conjunction of fortune and friendship.

The stream of my life had been gathering force. The exhibits in the library had attracted faculty interest to the degree that the Academic Senate Library Committee's annual report for the year 1939–40 cited them as outstanding. An article about them appeared in the UCLA alumni magazine. Other articles and monographs had brought modest recognition in the fields of bibliography, literature, and history. In 1942 Randolph Adams wrote several times of library positions he had recommended me for: the Library Company of Philadelphia, the Wrenn Library at the University of Texas, as successor to Fanny Ratchford, and a position under MacLeish in the Library of Congress.

Closer to home, Henry R. Wagner, the historian and bibliographer, another acquaintance from the job with Jake Zeitlin, recommended me variously to succeed Lawrence C. Wroth at the John Carter Brown Library, Herbert I. Priestley at the Bancroft Library, and the Librarian of Pomona College.

The curator of UCLA's William Andrews Clark Memorial Library, the gracious Cora E. Sanders, was due to retire at the end of 1943. President Sproul had appointed a committee to recommend her successor. It was composed of Louis B. Wright of the Huntington Library, who taught bibliography at UCLA, Waldemar Westergaard, UCLA history professor, with whom I had arranged the Hersholt-Andersen exhibit, and Sigurd B. Hustvedt, a dour Scandinavian professor of English at UCLA. Wright and Westergaard wanted me. Hustvedt wanted the elderly retiring head of the Philadelphia Library Company, whose passiveness would allow Hustvedt to continue to dominate the book ordering at the Clark. My knowledge of the Clark's strength was derived from its orders being placed through the UCLA department, where I was assigned to check them. As a result of committee disagreement, nothing was happening, a common thing when academic committees were involved.

The Haynes Foundation of Los Angeles wanted to commission a biography of its founder, Dr. John R. Haynes, a local political reformer. My book on Pickett, California's pioneer reformer, made me a natural choice. Here again there was indecisiveness and inaction. Katherine Anderson, my former library school teacher, wrote from Portland that she had urged President Sproul to appoint me to succeed Sydney Mitchell when he retired as dean of the school.

So 1942 passed and the heavens were filled with these shooting stars, each one brighter than the one before. They all flared and burned out. I continued to work for $155 a month, typing, and checking, and stamping books, arranging displays, and writing steadily on one topic or another when night had come.

As the war deepened, I felt guilty at being in non-essential work. A weak back made me unfit for military service. I wrote to the Greyhound Bus Company to apply for a job as a driver, and was given an appointment for interview when, in the spring of 1943, the heavens lit up again. In rapid succession I received letters from Bill Jackson, Randolph Adams, and Louis Wright, all saying that they had recommended me to succeed the late Theodore W. Koch as librarian of Northwestern University in Evanston, Illinois.

It had begun at a dinner party at the Jacksons' apartment in Cambridge. Present were Professor E. N. Hooker of UCLA, engaged upon a monumental editing of Dryden and Professor Leon Howard of Northwestern, who mentioned to Jackson and Hooker his institution's need of a new university librarian. Hooker and Jackson recommended me. When the university wrote to Adams, he did likewise; and in turning down the position when it had first been offered to him, Wright had named me as his choice.

On July 20, 1943, Professor Homer D. Vanderblue, Dean of Northwestern's College of Commerce and bibliographer of Adam Smith, wrote and invited me to come back for interview by his committee of selection and by the President of Northwestern, Franklyn D. Snyder.

I did not seek an appointment with either Goodwin or Sproul, but applied for my annual vacation and sought a train reservation to Chicago. Wartime made civilian travel virtually impossible. It was friendship that did it. Charles K. Adams, assistant freight agent of the Santa Fe, was a member of the Zamorano Club of Los Angeles, to which I had been elected in 1941. I phoned him. Within the hour I had an upper berth on the *Super Chief*, leaving that evening. I wired Dean Vanderblue my time of arrival, cancelled my interview with Greyhound and upon Fay's strong urging, typed out my resignation, effective at the end of my month's vacation. I gave no reason; and as I entered Union Station to take the train, I dropped my resignation in the mailbox. If the university wanted me back, it would be only as successor to John E. Goodwin. Thus I crossed my Rubicon.

I felt free, as I sat in the diner that night, while the crack flyer snaked up through Cajon Pass. Dessert was blueberries and cream. It was the first time I had ridden the Santa Fe since those many childhood crossings between Washington and Pasadena.

All went well at Evanston. I loved the beautiful graystone Deering Library on the lakefront, the bookish treasures Koch, the bibliophile, had collected, the fireplace in his panelled office. There was a gracious lady acting as librarian. "Do come," she said. "We need you."

Vanderblue and his committee and Snyder were warmly persuasive. Nothing was agreed upon when I left for Los Angeles, but I knew the job was mine if I wanted it.

Back on campus, my resignation had created widespread faculty indignation. Many wrote to President Sproul, urging him to bring me back. Goodwin, I learned later, had written in relief to Dean Mitchell, "The young man has resigned and things have calmed down."

I asked for an appointment with President Sproul. He greeted me with his characteristic laugh. "Powell," he said, "I haven't had such a snowstorm of letters since the Beecroft case." He was referring to a young political science instructor the old guard had dumped a few years before.

I grinned.

"You've been to Evanston?"

"Just came back."

"Do you want to work there?"

"Not if UCLA wants me."

"But not as junior librarian, I take it."

"No sir, nor as senior librarian."

"As University Librarian?"

"Yes."

"How long do I have?"

"President Snyder said he would present my name to the Trustees when they meet three weeks from now."

"Good," Sproul said. "I'll get busy."

He did. He asked the Senate Budget Committee to recommend a faculty committee to name a successor to Goodwin. I began work on a concrete storm drain to carry the Beverly Glen creek through our front yard without washing out our garage, as it had almost done the winter before.

The committee was appointed by Sproul, and it was blue ribbon. Composed of elder statesmen, it was chaired by Professor Westergaard, and included César Barja, professor of Spanish, U. S. Grant IV, professor of geology, Martin Huberty, professor of irrigation engineering, and Sigurd B. Hustvedt, my Clark Library nemesis.

As his personal representative on the committee, Sproul named Lindley Bynum, his special assistant in charge of library field collecting. This was the legendary paisano, "Pinky" Bynum, who when the Huntington Library had let him go as their field man, had been snapped up by Sproul. Bibliophile, vinophile, raconteur, ballad singer, and what have you, Bynum was another Zeitlin-era acquaintance who had been won by my book on Jeffers. Since coming to UCLA he and I had become friends; and one day he had confessed to me that he had first thought of himself as successor to Goodwin, but on thinking it over he realized that he would have to work too hard. Observing my willingness to do so, he had decided to back me for the job.

I couldn't have had a better committee if I had picked it myself. Even Hustvedt was for me, believing that as University Librarian I would be eliminated as a Clark Library contender, thereby enabling him to place his choice in the position.

I proceeded to build forms, mix and pour concrete, keeping away from campus. Bynum and I were in touch each night by phone. The committee was going to interview at least two other candidates, both men with administrative experience. My interview was due any day. Fay called to me one morning, in the midst of the last mix on the storm drain. "It's Pinky. The committee wants you to come right over."

"I can't leave," I replied. "This mix has to be poured or I'll lose it."

She went back to the phone, and returned in a moment, coming out to where I was adding sand and cement, gravel, and water.

"Pinky says it's urgent."

I mopped my brow.

"Tell him I'll come at two this afternoon."

I don't know what she told Bynum, but I do know that when I entered the committee room that afternoon, freshly shaved and showered, I was greeted first by Professor Huberty, the irrigation expert, who remarked solemnly, "The committee wishes to inspect your masterpiece. It must be a marvel."

There was laughter, as I held out my calloused hands.

"I apologize, gentlemen, but I just couldn't waste that last batch."

Each member questioned me in turn. I had answers for each, knowing their special interests, as well as the general interest and need. From five and a half years in the library I knew what it needed. In a dime notebook I had written down from time to time what I thought should be done in the way of changes and improvements.

My administrative inexperience never came up. I was relaxed and confident in the atmosphere of good humor. It was also helpful that I had once done a favor for Professor Grant, grandson of the President, when early in my work at UCLA he had mistaken me for a student and drafted me to unload his carful of books being given to the library. Westergaard told me later that after I had left the room and he was polling the committee, all Grant said was, "He can sure carry his weight in books." Bynum phoned that night and reported a unanimous vote in my favor.

Then nothing happened. Neither Bynum nor Westergaard would explain the silence from the President. Bynum came up one evening and said, "Westy wonders if you would be willing to take the associate librarianship if the committee were to recommend Jens Nyholm as Head Librarian."

I saw through Westergaard's desire to have a fellow Scandinavian whom he could more closely control. I sent a night letter to Sproul, demanding action. When I showed the copy next morning to Pinky, he groaned, "Oh my God, the prexy will blow his top when he reads this."

He didn't. Sproul wired back, reminding me that I had given him three weeks, and that only nineteen days had passed. He went on to ask me to come to Berkeley at his expense the following week to discuss the matter.

The university obtained travel priority for me and I took the overnight *Owl* to Berkeley. Again I was heartily greeted by RGS.

"Well, do you have your offer from Northwestern?"

"I do, to begin on January 1." I did not add that the offer was not yet in writing.

"I can now offer you a choice of positions. The Clark Library, beginning January 1, when Miss Sanders retires; or the University Library next July 1, when Mr. Goodwin retires. Which do you prefer?"

My reply took the genial look from Sproul's face.

"Both," I said.

"Both?" he asked.

"As Director of the Clark and as University Librarian, I can give them the coordination they need."

I knew that I had caught his interest. He saw a fiscal saving with the two positions on a single salary; and he asked me to enlarge on the idea. I did and to his satisfaction, and then we negotiated the salary. The Clark to be $4,000 as of January, the double salary to be $6,000 on July 1.

"What will you do till January?" he asked me. It was then early September.

"Work in a war plant. My brother is in charge of a factory producing kapok life jackets for the Navy and arctic sleeping bags for the Army."

I saw Sproul again a week later in Los Angeles, after the Regents had acted favorably on my appointments.

"What did Mr. Goodwin say?" I asked.

"He nearly had a stroke."

Not only was he angry with me, I heard, but he also felt he had been slapped by his oldest colleagues.

The word was out, for I had insisted that the university make the announcement at once and not wait until January. Now the faculty letters snowed on me. But not from Hustvedt. Years passed before he would speak to me. Then, after he had retired and was unable to exist on an inadequate pension, I was able to get him appointed at the Clark as a special assistant on the Dryden project. It was the first time he had been back to the Clark in several years. At first he didn't speak to me. He did something better. A sweet smile crossed his face.

When I finally said No to President Synder, I recommended Jens Nyholm for the job. He got it and has been at Northwestern ever since.

Upon leaving President Sproul's office on the Berkeley campus, I went to Dean Mitchell. It was our first meeting since 1939, nor had we corresponded. He had written me off.

He had, of course, heard from Goodwin of my resignation and that I had gone to Northwestern. He did not disguise his astonishment, as I brought him up to date. Mitchell was a realist. The king is dead, long live the king. He leaned his head to mine and we began the professional collaboration that lasted until his death seven or eight years later. We agreed on the need for a President's Committee of University of California head librarians, to include, of course, the Dean of the Library School. Then and there the Library Council was conceived, now nearing its first quarter-century of service to the statewide university libraries. I never blamed Mitchell for not recognizing my administrative potential. Few did. In fact I was the only one who fully realized it. Now it was up to me to develop it.

A BREATHING SPELL

The ensuing four-months' "breather" was just what was needed to free me from tension and lend perspective on the work ahead. It was good to continue the physical activity I had benefitted from in making the storm drain, a crude affair, true, but built to outlast Hadrian's Wall. Our Glen neighbor, a building contractor who had advised me in planning the work, kept telling me I was overbuilding it. I had paid no attention, and shovelled in ever richer amounts of cement, sand, and gravel, reinforcing the forms with steel twice as heavy as necessary.

The war plant in which I was employed as a common laborer at $1.00 an hour was in the central manufacturing district, twenty-eight miles from home. I left before daylight each morning at 5:45 and was at work by 7:00. My job was to unload 300-lb. Java kapok bales from freight cars alongside the plant, wheel them to a grinder, cut the baling wire, strip off the woven mat wrapping, then peel out the long flat ribbons of creamy kapok, for all the world like animal fur, and feed them evenly into the powerful electric machine which shredded the kapok, eliminated the black seeds, and passed the airy material into a blowing chamber on the other side of which two men, using nozzled hoses, fired the stuff into the empty life jackets. It was a dangerous job for those men, as shredded kapok is inflammable. The walls of the blowing room were of flimsy material, so that if there was an explosion—and there were several—the men could roll to safety as an automatic fire extinguishing system came into action.

For a 130-lb. man to handle 300-lb. bales meant skill in leverage and balance, rather than strength. Once learned, I got along nicely.

The half-hour lunch period was divided between tuna sandwiches on whole-wheat buns and a thermos of tea, packed by Fay, while I read in *Old Calabria* and *Fountains in the Sand*, two of Norman Douglas' evocative travel books; and crap shooting with my fellow laborers, Mexicans and Negroes, on the floor of one of the emptied boxcars. I was a good crapshooter, having learned the art, extracurricular, in high school, and I won consistently. The Professor, they called me, and begged me to reveal my system. Go to church on Sundays, I told them. Winnings were spent on the way home at a supermarket atop the hill on Slauson Boulevard, and for luxuries we could not afford on my $1.00 an hour: olive oil, steaks, butter, wine and cigarettes for Fay, at least when war shortages permitted.

By this time I neither drank nor smoked. The latter I gave up on the first day of library school in 1936 when, after I lit a cigarette in class, Miss Sisler reproved me as though I were a naughty boy, not a graduate student. Always one for the dramatic gesture, I tore my pack to shreds, and announced "Henceforth, I shall be pure as the driven snow." And I have not smoked again.

Stopping drinking was not as easy. I failed a couple of times, although I knew I must succeed if I were to keep my health and rise in the profession. My equilibrium was such that increasingly small amounts of alcohol, even in wine and beer, disturbed it. Besides, I was naturally "high," Fay used to say, and alcohol blew me right out of my skin. I had no more driving accidents, but I did some damn fool things. Once at a party given by Jens Nyholm, before he went to Berkeley, I spun around the room in an exuberant solo dance, lost my balance, and sat down with a crash on the "Great Dane's" new glass coffee table, spread with open-face sandwiches. I sat there in the ruins, looking up at Nyholm's tragic face, and true to my philosophy of "attack, never retreat," I berated him for having such a fragile piece of furniture. I felt that I had partly made amends when I recommended him to Northwestern.

It was not until New Year's Eve, 1938, in our Sherman Oaks home, the Ritchies, Newells, and Eversons, gathered for a cooperative celebration, each couple bringing food and drinks, that I received the news from my sister-in-law in South Africa that Clark had died of a fractured skull following an accidental fall on the stone steps of Transvaal University College. He was only thirty-eight and already an authority on citrus growing in the Commonwealth. I was proud rather than fond of him. Then and there I decided to do something in his memory, something noble. Without revealing the contents of the cable, I announced to friends and Fay that I had gone on the wagon. Wait till morning! they cried. No, I said, now, or never! And that's how it was.

Being a teetotaller is a disadvantage when other people are drinking, for one remains sober as others become garrulous, even foolish. For protection at faculty and other parties when the liquor was flowing, I would sit down at the piano, thus giving both myself and others pleasure. I also overheard academic indiscretions which sometimes proved useful.

We entertained constantly during those years in Beverly Glen, Fay having become a superb cook and also able to get the most out of our limited budget. The boys always helped, making place cards, parking cars, and being part of the group. We organized hiking cookouts, the guests arriving in the afternoon, having been warned to wear old clothes; whereupon the boys and I would lead them up a hogback to a ridge trail and down to the Stone Canyon Reservoir and back by another route to find Fay and the women guests uncapping beer and preparing to grill hamburgers over charcoal. Once it was a party for redheaded men and their wives. Wayland Hand, Samuel Herrick, James Gilluly, Alonzo Cass, Hugh Miller, and of course "Pinky" Bynum. I'll never forget their faces as they looked at each other when all had arrived, and realized what had happened.

In 1941 I had started to write novels again. Henry Miller was our neighbor, and I was bringing him a steady supply of reading matter from the UCLA Library. He was encouraging me to persist as a writer. Dr. Bieler and I lunched together once a week, when he called on patients in Beverly Hills and Westwood, and he too urged me to keep writing so-called creative works. In the autumn of 1943 even the demands of the long drive and the heavy work at the plant did not drain away my strength. I began a long college novel and wrote on it every night for an hour or two before falling asleep.

I was ready, physically and mentally, for the assignments Sproul had given me, and on January 2, I reported for work at the Clark Library, reported to myself: for the first time I was in charge. The retiring Miss Sanders stayed on a week and gave me helpful orientation. The small staff of librarians, gardeners, and custodians, offered me every cooperation, as I began a directorship that lasted nearly twenty-three years.

The Clark Library had belonged to UCLA for ten years, since the death of William Andrews Clark, Jr. had brought it and an endowment of $1,500,000 to UCLA, and although the book collections had benefitted from Miss Sanders' and Professor Hustvedt's meaningful acquisitions, nothing else had happened. The place was an imposing mausoleum. Many people proposed uses for the library and grounds, but as chairman of the Library Committee, President Sproul ruled that none of them were in harmony with the Deed of Gift. There was a power vacuum and no one to fill it.

Although on the committee, Goodwin looked to the faculty members for action. The various conflicting moves they proposed were checkmated by the President. Until Hustvedt came on the committee and, together with Miss Sanders, began to concentrate buying in the Dryden period, the library's greatest strength, there was no agreement on what area to develop. One professor favored Western Americana, another the Napoleonic era, still another American literature. Another suggestion was to make the Clark a typographical museum, installing therein as curator the eminent type designer Frederick Goudy. The Clark with its rich endowment was a plum that tempted many to grab for it. Goodwin's greatest contribution was to employ Frank A. Lundy to inventory and catalog the collection.

Sproul saw in me the first person who seemed capable of taking the Clark in hand and developing it in keeping with the founder's wishes, that it be a research collection to serve UCLA's scholars and students. At our September meeting he had requested me to prepare a program for the Clark's development, and soon after I had taken office, Sproul convened the Clark committee to hear what I proposed. I had read through the Deed of Gift and all the correspondence and committee minutes for the past decade, talked with Miss Sanders and with members of the faculty, particularly with Professor E. N. Hooker, the Dryden scholar. I knew what should be done and I had plans for doing it: more concentrated acquisitions, publications of a faculty-staff report on the library's first ten years, the establishment of graduate fellowships, and an annual open house to be known as Founder's Day.

I requested also a free hand in purchasing, instead of the cumbersome procedure of submitting lists to the committee for advance approval. Finally, I proposed the appointment of a bibliographical assistant who would be in immediate charge when, as University Librarian, I would be required to spend most of my time on campus.

The committee heard me elaborate on the typed outline I had given them, and then they put questions to me. In addition to President Sproul, the membership included Bynum, Professor Frank J. Klingberg, Professor Dixon Wecter, both staunch friends, and Professor Hustvedt. The latter remained silent and stony-faced until President Sproul, knowing what would follow, called for a unanimous vote of approval.

"It seems to me a rather sweeping transfer of authority," Hustvedt said, "from the committee to the Director."

"Are you ready to vote, gentlemen?" the President asked.

All but Hustvedt responded with aye.

The President bore down. "Does Professor Hustvedt wish the minutes to show that he abstained from voting?"

"Make it unanimous," he murmured.

Hustvedt resigned from the committee soon after and was replaced by Professor Hooker.

That was the only untoward incident of my long directorship. The Clark owes an enormous debt to Robert Gordon Sproul for having dominated the library until a meaningful program could be proposed and approved.

The next meeting of a crucial nature was of the Regents Committee on Southern California campuses, which Sproul convened at the Clark. It included two friends who never failed to support me throughout my career. The first was Edward A. Dickson, the Los Angeles newspaperman, who had served as a Regent since 1913 and who, with Provost Ernest Carroll Moore, was the inspired architect of UCLA's phenomenal rise. He and my father had been friends and when they were both stationed in Washington during the war, my father, as chief executive of Sunkist, had choice Riverside navels delivered regularly to Mr. and Mrs. Dickson's suite in the Mayflower Hotel. The Dicksons never tired of telling me of this courtesy. I learned later, from another source, that the Regent's post held so long by Mr. Dickson had first been offered to my father by Governor Stephens, but that my father, then new at Sunkist, had decided that he could not give the necessary time to the university post and had declined. He had also declined the deanship of the College of Agriculture at Berkeley, saying that his heart belonged first to Southern California.

The other friend on the Board of Regents was Edwin A. Pauley, the oilman, who had preceded me at Occidental as a member of Owl and Key and then had been a fraternity brother of George's at Stanford. It did not matter that Ed Pauley called me Larry one day and Jerry (for George) the next, he always knew I was a Powell.

Thus the Regents Committee meeting was *pro forma*. As chairman, Dickson proposed blanket approval of my present and future proposals. It was seconded by Pauley, and the committee adjourned for tea in the drawing room.

My bibliographical assistant was the first of a series of library protégés I nurtured at the two libraries. He was H. Richard Archer, a promising young bookman who was clerking on Sixth Street in another bookstore at the time I was working for Jake Zeitlin. My going into library work showed him the way, but first he had to finish the last two years of his A.B. at Berkeley before entering library school. Upon completing both courses, he had gone on to the University of Chicago's Graduate Library School for the Ph.D. We had been in touch throughout his education and I knew he was my man for the Clark post. After eight years at Clark, Archer returned to Chicago to complete his Ph.D. and go on to become librarian of the Lakeside Press, and finally the curator of the Chapin Library at Williams College.

During our years at the Clark, Archer and I worked together with good results, simplifying procedures, buying with the flair we both had for antiquarian materials, and in particular, developing the graphic arts collection, notably Southern California printers and Eric Gill.

Those first six months at the Clark were a honeymoon. For the first time I savored the joys of being my own boss, with a mandate to do what was necessary. I grew to love that elegant place, the serene building and its great books, the formal gardens so beautifully tended, the whole forming an oasis in the traffic-howling wilderness of Los Angeles. I read constantly in the twin fields of the library's strength: the age of Dryden and the age of Wilde. The Zamorano Club held an evening meeting at the Clark, and the oak-panelled drawing room gleamed with light from tapers in candelabras of sterling silver. At Founder's Day in June, held in collaboration with UCLA alumni homecoming, we staged an outdoor pageant for 1,500 guests: period music by faculty players and a ballad opera, *The Devil to Pay*, directed by Ralph Freud and played by Professors Dudley Pegrum and Jesse Bond. It was a triumph, repeated annually for half a dozen years, when John Dryden and Oscar Wilde, Handel and Purcell were played and sung. The Clark Library was brought into the community and campus cultural stream, each year enlarging and refining its program until it became a beehive of scholarly and aesthetic activity.

Freed by Sproul from having to gain committee approval of every administrative detail, I was able to proceed rapidly to carry out the widening new program. Thousands of religious and political tracts were added. Early English science was collected, including what came to be a massive assemblage of the 17th-century works of Robert Boyle, the father of chemistry. Today the Clark's early science collection is the best in the western United States.

In that halcyon spring I continued to work on the novel evenings. Gordon Newell, his wife and their two children had returned to Los Angeles from Big Sur. He had just quit a job in a plastics factory when Emelia's handmade jewelry began to bring in sufficient income so that he could give full time to wood- and stone-carving. I would go to his studio near the Clark with my lunch and while he worked on various projects, I would read aloud from my work in progress. It was a repetition of the experience we had fourteen years before in Carmel, that golden time when my Jeffers project was born.

Ritchie had been forced to take leave from his Press, when paper and metal shortages curtailed production, and to take a job at the Douglas Aircraft Plant, in charge of their printed forms. I had come close to the Ward Ritchie Press in the years from its founding and had collected every book, pamphlet and scrap the Press had issued. This collection was presented to the Clark Library at another evening meeting of the Zamorano Club at which a paper was read on Ritchie's work.

The Clark Library now has an example also of Gordon Newell's sculpture. In the last days of my directorship I had a cast intaglio relief of a flute player inset in the garden wall. Newell had given it to me on one of those lunchtime visits in 1944.

It was a rich spring, during which I gained the necessary knowledge of university administrative procedures that would serve me when I became University Librarian. I made a point of knowing the key people in purchasing, business, accounting, grounds and buildings, and personnel, finding fortunately that the manager of the latter office, Mildred Foreman, had been an Occidental classmate.

I also held two all-important interviews, of a woman and a man whose careers and mine were henceforth to be twined. The first was for the secretary I would require on campus. Miss Foreman knew my need. She sent Miss Elizabeth Steward Bradstreet who was to rise to be my senior administrative assistant and remain during the seventeen years of my tenure. A tall, poised, brown-haired, blue-eyed Maine Yankee, cordial, shrewd, discreet, and above all loyal, Braddie was God-sent. She had worked as Goodwin's secretary for only a few months, not long enough to develop an attachment that could not be transferred to me. She would be able to fill me in about staff and budget.

When Miss Bradstreet came to the Clark for an interview, I learned that her work had been mostly for the head of the order department, my old supervisor, who planned to leave when Goodwin did, and that Goodwin's activity had slowed down so that he required almost no secretarial assistance. She was pleased when I said that I would not only want her full time to type my work, but I was sure we would need additional help. My feeling about her warmed when I learned that she also had had accounting experience and could take charge of the library budget. She said very little about Goodwin, nor did I try to pump her. What she did say was sad—that he spent most of the days now seated at his desk, looking out the window.

The other interview was to find a replacement for the order department supervisor. I knew from the first that if she didn't leave, I would have to find her another position. Now my only problem was that of replacing her. Mitchell solved my problem. "Just the man for you," he wrote, "he'll be as good in his way on campus as Archer will be at the Clark." This candidate was at Stanford as a junior reference librarian the previous two years, and the two before that he had spent after graduation from the Berkeley library school as a junior acquisitions librarian under Leupp at Cal. Mitchell enclosed the candidate's picture. One look at Robert Vosper and I knew, even before I had met him, that he was my man. He proved it in the eight years we worked together. And more than my man—a man of the profession at large, rising to head the ALA and eventually to succeed me as both University Librarian and Director of the Clark Library.

Vosper came south in the spring of 1944, arriving at the Clark as Miss Bradstreet was leaving, and we spent the day and the evening together, as I took him home for a family dinner. The job, as we both saw it, was for a collection builder, an acquisitions not an accessions librarian. I promised him a free hand in book selection. It did not matter to me that he had never selected books, any more than it mattered to him that I had never headed a university library. Each had confidence in the other.

I could not have succeeded without those two key persons. They proved indispensable to me and I came to cherish them both.

MY TEN-CENT NOTEBOOK

During the last week in June, 1944, I went to Berkeley and called on every office whose help I might need—purchasing, personnel, architects and engineers, and University Press. At that time the Los Angeles campus was still tied to Berkeley in many ways. Sproul was the boss of both campuses, having removed the UCLA provost, Ernest Carroll Moore, from office in 1936 and then appointed an interim provost, the mathematician Earl Hedrick. When Hedrick died, Sproul filled the office himself and so until Clarence Dykstra came as provost in 1945, I reported directly to Sproul, who spent most of his time at Berkeley.

If UCLA was still subservient, the situation was better than Goodwin had found it when he became University Librarian in 1923. At that time all book purchases for UCLA were placed through the library at Berkeley, and the policy was to limit UCLA to 100,000 volumes. Then in his prime, Goodwin was able to break these restrictions and also to plan the monumental library building occupied in 1929 upon the move to the new campus at

Westwood. This rebelliousness on his part was why Leupp despised Goodwin and, I believe, had never visited the Westwood campus.

Leupp was at home recovering from a cold when I arrived in Berkeley on my peace mission, and I phoned to ask if I might visit him. I received a cordial welcome from the old tyrant, relaxed and mellow in his own home, pleased I am sure by the knowledge that I was not Goodwin's choice to succeed him. I had come to talk of the need for a statewide classification and pay plan for library personnel, the number one item in my dime notebook. "Wait six months," Leupp urged, "and take it up with my successor."

I had already met his successor-designate, Donald Coney, Librarian of the University of Texas, who had come through Los Angeles a few months before on his way from Austin to Berkeley for an interview. When he was having difficulty getting a train reservation on the last lap from Los Angeles, Sproul's secretary had phoned, saying she knew I had influence somewhere in railroad circles and would I use it to get Coney moved along. Again my friend Charles K. Adams acted.

I met Coney when he arrived on the *Sunset Limited* in the morning and we spent the day together until I put him on the *Owl* that night. I found him shrewd, witty, dry but not dull, and we agreed on everything that related to library cooperation in the new era, chiefly Mitchell's and my idea of a Library Council. It was an important meeting for the libraries we were to head. We proved harmonious. I tried never to allow my aggressive actions on behalf of UCLA to jeopardize my relationship with Coney. We were frank with each other. He was as necessary for Berkeley in his time as I was for UCLA.

I can give an example of the way Coney and I worked together. At the end of the war, when he and I were at the beginning of our tenures, I received a phone call from President Sproul, asking me how much money it would take to acquire those wartime continental imprints we had been unable to buy during the hostilities.

"May I call you back tomorrow?" I said, intending to ask Vosper to make a crash estimate.

"I am going into a Regents Finance Committee meeting in twenty minutes," was the answer.

I took a deep breath and said, "Fifty thousand dollars."

The phone clicked in my ear.

A few minutes later a call came in from Coney. "Did the President call you?" he asked.

"Yes. Did he call you?"

"Yes."

We both waited. Then Coney asked, "How much did you tell him?"

"Fifty thousand. How much did you?"

There was a dry laugh, then Coney said, "Fifty thousand."

We both laughed and hung up. And we got $50,000 each and spent it.

I suspect that someday the Berkeley administration will be brought to judgment eventually for having booted away the gift of the greatest Americana library of our time, the collection of Thomas W. Streeter, offered by him with only two conditions, that it be kept together as an integral part of the Bancroft Library and that the university spend an annual minimum of $25,000 to enlarge it. Unable to obtain agreement between Coney and Bancroft Director George P. Hammond, President Sproul, after an initial visit to Streeter at Morristown, New Jersey, ignored the offer. Following the death of Streeter, his peerless collection is being auctioned and it is estimated that it may realize as much as $10,000,000.

I returned to campus on July 1, the first time I had set foot there since my September conference with Sproul.

I was not given any welcome by the staff. Their attitude was one of watchful waiting. Rumors had spread, of wholesale firing, reshuffling of positions, and the like. The one exception was a gesture on the part of Rudolph Engelbarts, a junior cataloger. He and his wife had a potted plant placed in my office. Of course Miss Bradstreet welcomed me with open pad and sharpened pencil. I sat down in Goodwin's chair and looked fixedly out the window. We laughed, then went to work—and didn't stop for seventeen years.

Goodwin had departed the night before, taking with him personal papers. Otherwise he left everything the way it had always been. The first thing I did was to read through the files of correspondence, personnel folders, and Library Committee minutes. This took a week or two. There was not much. Goodwin was a man of few words, either written or spoken.

I did remember to go next door and introduce Vosper to his department (my old department); and then I walked through the building and called on friend and foe alike. Three of the younger women, who were nevertheless old in seniority, were with me: Deborah King, head of the Reserved Book Room, Gladys Coryell, supervisor of the Graduate Reading Room, and Ardis Lodge, a junior reference librarian. The head reference librarian, Fanny Alice Coldren, although one of the old guard and destined to retire in two more years to become the widower Goodwin's second wife, proved herself a professional person of highest character, for though I knew she never liked me, she was punctilious in respect to me and devotion to the library and the new policies.

I called a staff meeting and told them of my general plans, including first of all (upon the arrival of Donald Coney at Berkeley) to reclassify and remunerate their positions. Really nothing more than that was needed to win their support; and furthermore that I would appoint a staff committee to counsel me in the reclassification study. The committee consisted of Vosper, Miss Lodge and Miss Jeannette Hagan, a junior cataloger, who had come up through the ranks. The professional-clerical ratio was grossly out of balance, with approximately thirty professionals and five clericals. This meant that professional librarians were engaged in work that required only clerical, even student assistance. Staff morale was understandably low.

The other front on which I had to make peace was that of the faculty, as represented by its Senate Library Committee. Although a member of the Senate, the Librarian was not a member of the committee, serving rather as its nonvoting secretary. This I never changed, finding it desirable to use the committee as a shield, always being able to disassociate myself from its actions. The major responsibilities of the committee were to participate with the Librarian in the allocation of the book budget and the assignment of library space. It did not operate in the areas of staffing and service and I did not propose to let it do so.

I can give an illustration of the advantages to the librarian of a strong library committee. On almost my first day in office one of the faculty, not a member of the Library Committee, requested the use as a seminar room of an area to be relinquished by the shrinking Navy meteorological training program which, at the height of the war, had taken over much of the library's space. His argument was first come, first served. I said the matter would have to go to the Library Committee.

"So you are going to follow Goodwin's delaying policies, are you?"

"I'm going to respect the responsibility of the Senate's

Committee," I replied. "If the committee does not act according to your wishes, you are free to bring the matter to the Senate floor."

Had he been sent by the committee to test me? I never knew.

The chairman of the Library Committee, biochemist Max S. Dunn, had spread word by the grapevine that he was going to put the new librarian in his place. Dunn was angry about not having been named to the committee which selected me, and probably he should have been an ex officio member.

He arrived one day without notice, a gamecock of a man, smoking a cigar with such a rank smell that Miss Bradstreet told me afterward that he would either have to smoke finer cigars or she would leave.

"I'm glad you came," I said to Dunn before he could speak. "I need your advice."

I opened my dime notebook and began to read the list of things to be done. When I had finished, Dunn grinned, and thrust out his hand. "You've got a job ahead of you."

"What else is there to do?" I said, knowing that I had deliberately omitted the one thing Dunn had been angry with Goodwin about.

"The Library Committee believes that departmental book allocations should be common knowledge. Goodwin insisted that they be kept secret."

"I agree and also that the committee's minutes should be open to all."

"Now let's not go *too* far," Dunn cautioned.

Max Dunn and I were friends from then on, as I was with later committee chairmen, until the end of my tenure when I fell out with my old colleague, the redheaded party guest, astronomer Samuel Herrick, a scholar, not an administrator.

The faculty was starved for information about library

policy and plans. And so was the library staff. Good-win's drift was to do little and tell nothing. I began a chatty series called "The Librarian's Occasional Letter to the Faculty" and encouraged Vosper to issue a serial called "Acquisition Notes," written by faculty and staff members on important purchases and gifts.

Vosper also began a round of talks with faculty members which led to his drafting an acquisitions code, a statement of the subjects and areas of knowledge which the library intended to develop. Vosper also worked with the Library Committee on better ways of allocating the book budget. The war had cut it to a low of $55,000 and we began the long effort to get the funds required, if the faculty was to have a library commensurate with its needs. In seventeen years the budget topped $1,000,-000, but it was a fight all the way, for it was never allowed to surpass Berkeley's and Coney did not show the same willingness to press for more money. He already had it, plus the benefit of Berkeley's long established international exchanges program.

In the beginning, book selection was entirely in faculty hands, except for the reference collection which Miss Coldren was building with great distinction. The Accessions Department's name was promptly changed to Acquisitions, but, except for Vosper, was not staffed with librarians either able or willing to engage in book selection. As the collections grew and faculty recommendations increasingly duplicated books already acquired, selection authority gradually came to the library. I continued to employ more bibliographical experts, of whom Vosper and Archer were the first.

It was evident from the first day that I had a jewel in Vosper. His quiet, pipe-smoking, unhurried way of working pleased faculty and staff alike. Whatever he did, he did with ease and grace. I have never known anyone else who turned out such amounts of finished work of every kind without ever seeming to exert himself. He forgot nothing, but never took notes. He could dictate or write a polished first draft, whereas I had to labor nearly endlessly over everything I wrote—and still do.

Vosper demonstrated his worth in the profession when he was sent to represent the library at exchanges conferences in Mexico City and at Princeton. After the latter meeting Coney spoke warmly of Vosper's performance. This was high praise. In all my years of work with Coney, I rarely heard him speak with extra warmth of anyone, and the times he did, it was of my chief assistants such as Vosper, Neal Harlow, Andrew Horn, Gordon Williams, and Page Ackerman, which of course pleased me all the more.

The Library Council was established by President Sproul in advance of Coney's appointment, and the first meeting was held at Santa Barbara, the University's newest campus. Mitchell and I and Mt. Hamilton's Fritz Neubauer, the astronomer-librarian, were the only men in attendance, Leupp being indisposed. The San Francisco Medical Librarian, the legendary John B. de C. M. Saunders, F.R.C.S., came regularly to later meetings when he learned that he could find kindred spirits there. The women who attended the inaugural meeting included Nell Branch, Davis; Margaret Buvens, Riverside; and Ruth Ragan, La Jolla.

In addition to recommending that President Sproul initiate the class-pay study, the Council asked for a survey of the statewide libraries' book holdings. Mitchell had an *arrière pensée* in supporting this, for his erstwhile protégé, Dr. Fulmer Mood, needed a job. Mood was a Harvard Ph.D. in history Mitchell had trained at library school, sent to Redlands as librarian, then brought back as his heir apparent. Mood proved unable as a teacher to gain student approval. They all but mutinied against

Mitchell's choice. We believed Mood's research talents would lend themselves to the proposed library survey. He was appointed and in two years' time he produced an enormous manuscript which collapsed under its own weight. It proved too big a task to accomplish by ordinary historical and comparative means. The survey was filed away and forgotten. I found Mood a charming crotchet, filled with odd bits and pieces of learning. He ambled from campus to campus, making friends and enemies with equal impartiality, developing a theory of comparison by a linear measurement of the several shelf lists. It always seemed to reveal that Berkeley had so many feet, UCLA so many inches, and the other campuses a few centimeters. My faculty rejected it utterly.

Also high on the list in my 10¢ notebook was the need to decentralize the library's collections and services. At the Westergaard Committee interview this was strongly urged by Professor Huberty. His department, Agriculture, Chemistry under Dunn, and Geology, all three upon being denied branch libraries by Goodwin, had "bootlegged" departmental libraries, funded and staffed departmentally, independent of the central library. All three preferred, however, to have the library be responsible for acquiring, cataloging, and giving public service, and this we took steps to do. So that when after the war the first three of the professional schools came to campus in rapid succession, I was in a position to say to the President and their deans that the University Librarian should be given responsibility for establishing and managing their libraries. This meant that we had the opportunity to found collections and services for the Big Three: Engineering, Medicine, and Law.

This was made possible by employing unusual persons in these fields and then giving them authority, funds, and support. For Engineering Johanna Allerding was persuaded to leave the Pacific Aeronautical Library. She was a German girl who had been a classmate at library school, where I had been impressed by her thoroughness and her strong character. She needed both, for Dean Boelter of Engineering was a kind of human bulldozer, tough as nails and humorless.

The choice for Medicine, Louise Darling, I had known as a fellow junior in the early years at UCLA. Among my other duties, I also had the one of shipping clerk for the Accessions Department. Miss Darling also had the clerical job of wrapping interlibrary loans for the Reference Department. We would meet in the Receiving Room, and I never forgot the passion with which she would wrap and tie a parcel, as I got my finger off the knot just in time. I also remembered the way she walked about her work, moving with vigor along the shortest route between two points—and God help anyone who stood in her way. She had left to enter Army library work, and I reached her by phone in Manila, in time to divert her from an assignment that would have taken her for a year to Japan. Miss Darling had Spanish blood and her striking beauty and intense nature made her well liked by the doctors. She also had a steely will, not needed however in dealing with Dean Stafford Warren—for he was a great humanist, a Lincoln-like figure —but rather in coping with the problems of building from nothing a Biomedical Library to serve both the School of Medicine and the Life Sciences.

These two women did their jobs, built the libraries, and stayed with them, each becoming nationally recognized as a leader.

I was not so lucky in law. My initial choice of a librarian was good—Thomas S. Dabagh, the Armenian lawyer-librarian of the Los Angeles County Law Library. The Dean however was tricky, and when I went on sabbatical leave in 1950, he promptly told the Provost that I had agreed to let Law withdraw from the library system. Dabagh would not go along with this, resigned, and moved to Berkeley. The Dean continued on an aggressive course, and withdrew his faculty from the Senate. It was not until he was charged with anti-Semitic prejudice that his resignation followed. Thereupon, under the cordial Dean Richard Maxwell, the law faculty and library returned to the fold.

The branch library system was steadily developed, until it finally included eighteen units, all under the University Librarian, each with its own faculty library committee, and each professional school also represented on the Senate Library Committee.

This development demanded study, negotiation, and compromise, and it could not have been done without unusual staff and an enlightened administration and faculty.

When in 1946 Miss Coldren resigned to marry Goodwin, a key replacement was needed, that of Head Reference Librarian. I had in mind a former fellow student at Occidental, Everett T. Moore, who had gone on to Harvard for his M.A.; then when I was working at Zeitlin's, he taught at Webb School in Claremont and used to come in the shop on Saturdays to buy books and chat. Like Archer, Moore was inspired by my move to go to library school. He finished at Berkeley in 1939, then he and Vosper were juniors together on Leupp's staff, were both disillusioned and left, Moore going to the University of Illinois Library. From there he entered the Army, rising from truck driver to major. He came to UCLA directly from the Pacific theater, where he was on General MacArthur's staff. Everett Moore became a key member of the new staff, advancing in usefulness, taking charge of library editing and publications, and finally becoming a national spokesman for intellectual freedom.

Still another appointment, in 1945, brought Neal Harlow back to UCLA from where he had received his A.B. early in the 1930's, gone to the Berkeley library school, then became a Californiana expert, first in the Bancroft and then in the State Library at Sacramento. Soon after my appointment in 1944, Harlow wrote, proposing himself as candidate when a rare book or special collections librarian was needed. I brought him to the first opening, that of Gifts and Exchanges Librarian, and in his spare time, Harlow developed plans for Special Collections, eventually heading the new department. Dedication of the department in 1951 took the form of a symposium on "Rare Books and Research," addressed by Henry R. Wagner, George L. Harding, James T. Babb, Professors John Walton Caughey and Majl Ewing, and Neal Harlow.

In the meantime, as he showed a flair for the slide rule, Harlow, aided by Deborah King and Everett Moore, was given charge of the first major addition to the library, that of a four-story east wing. The war had delayed its construction, and in the postwar period, steel was in short supply; so that the library building expansion, both in public areas and stacks, never did catch up with need. We had to fight, clear to the legislature in Sacramento, for more book stacks, while Berkeley had no difficulty in expanding a library already twice the size of UCLA's. An uphill fight is always more fun, and when it is finally won, the celebration is that much more exuberant. And so it was.

The mid-forties also saw the appointment of two of the most bookish people I ever knew, both of whom stayed to make their careers at UCLA: Betty Rosenberg and Wilbur J. Smith.

In the summer of 1946 Andrew Horn came to my office for advice about going into library work. Andy Horn was no stranger to me, though I had never met

Two-year-old LCP with his mother, 1908

LCP's first speech, to his mother and brothers Clark and George, 1909

LCP at age 10, 1916

G. Harold Powell, LCP's father, 1920

"The Four Musketeers"
Groenewegen, Ritchie, LCP, and Newell, 1934

"The most exciting teacher . . .
I have ever known . . ."
C. F. McIntyre, 1930

College days, LCP and Fay, 1930

The Occidental College Jazz Band with LCP on piano, 1928

Dr. H. G. Bieler, "a friend of forty years"

Musician First Class LCP,
aboard the SS President
Harrison, 1925

Fay Powell with Professor Georges Connes

LCP at work, Paris, 1930

Prof. Jean Matruchot, "my best French friend," with LCP, 1931.
Matruchot introduced LCP to Henry Miller

Alfred Young Fisher, M. F. K. Fisher, and LCP, on the Riviera, 1932

LCP in Dijon, 1932

LCP between fellow students,
University of Dijon, 1931

Alfred Fisher and LCP, Dijon, 1931

Fay

A D. H. Lawrence-like LCP, Dijon, 1932

LCP and Fay are married on March 26, 1934 at the Ventura County
Court House. Left to Right: LCP, Fay, Edwina (Ted) Powell,
George Powell

LCP's sons Wilkie and Norman,
Easter, 1939

Fay by the hearth at Beverly Glen, 1940

LCP holds forth
to Luther Evans, 1949

LCP with U. of California
President Robert G. Sproul, 1945

"The UCLA Triumvirate"—Andrew Horn, LCP, Robert Vosper.
Above in 1949 and below at LCP's 1966 retirement

LCP with Henry Miller
at Big Sur, 1955

Left to right: Wilbur Smith,
J. E. Reynolds, Gordon Williams,
Richard O'Brien, LCP,
and (seated) Sol Malkin

Left to Right: Caroline Anderson,
LCP, Ward Ritchie

The UCLA School of Library Service Faculty and Staff, 1962: Seated, left to right: Elizabeth R. Baughman, Frances Clarke Sayers, Florence G. Williams, LCP, Andrew H. Horn, Barbara G. Boyd, Johanna E. Tallman, Gladys C. Graham. Standing, left to right: Wilma Dean, Louise Darling, Everett T. Moore, Mar Lynn Ormsby, James Sheehey, Betty Rosenberg, Seymour Lubetzky, Robert Vosper

Donald M. Powell and LCP at Tucson, 1953

LCP, Frances Clarke Sayers,
Jerome Cushman, 1965

Gardeners Fay and LCP, 1957

LCP in 1964
(ROBERT EISENBACH PHOTO)

Fay and LCP, Malibu, 1967   Ward Ritchie and LCP, 1967

Portraits of LCP and Fay by Netta Aldington

him, or even knew his name. I used to see him as a graduate student in history, joshing the girls, as I was checking order cards at the public catalog. He was a blond Swede. He wore rubber-soled shoes, a trench coat, and a crumpled felt hat.

After taking his Ph.D. in Medieval History Horn went into military service, then taught at Johns Hopkins, and now was drawn to library work. I tried him on a summer job on hourly wages, carding the large collection of foreign books bought en bloc after the war with the money Sproul had granted me. He did the job in record time, and it needed no revising. He went on to Berkeley—J. Periam Danton had succeeded Mitchell as Dean—and proved one of their most brilliant students. Harlow and I wanted Horn to be responsible for manuscripts in Special Collections. Coney also wanted Horn for his staff. We let Danton arbitrate and he ruled in favor of UCLA, and so Andy Horn returned to campus in 1948 as a senior librarian.

One of Horn's outstanding accomplishments at UCLA came soon after he had joined the staff. The Rosenbach Foundation's Freedom Train documents of great Americana were touring the country, and we arranged with Philip Rosenbach, the Doctor's elder brother who came regularly to Los Angeles to sell treasures to "Ma" Doheny, to hold an exhibition at UCLA. It represented a fortune in manuscripts and documents, including the *Bay Psalm Book*, the first book printed in the American colonies, and we took elaborate security and insurance safeguards. Aided by Edwin Carpenter, Horn was delegated to prepare a catalog of the exhibit, to be printed by Ward Ritchie at the Rosenbachs' expense. The two historian-librarians did so in record time, set up the exhibit; and we saw it draw record crowds, including a thief who nearly got away with the *Bay Psalm Book*.

In 1951 Vosper was promoted to Associate Librarian, Harlow to Assistant Librarian, and Horn to Head of Special Collections; and when Vosper and Harlow left to head the university libraries at Kansas and British Columbia, I promoted Horn, brought in Gordon Williams from the John Crerar Library as Assistant Librarians and made Wilbur Smith Head of Special Collections. Then when Horn went to North Carolina, Williams advanced and Miss Page Ackerman was jumped from a junior reference post to be Assistant Librarian, one of the best moves I ever made. She is now Vosper's Chief Associate Librarian. And finally, when Williams left to head the Midwest Inter-Library Center, Miss Ackerman moved up and Paul Miles was promoted to Assistant Librarian.

Before leaving for Chicago, Gordon Williams, whom I had recruited to library work from bookselling, planned the location and the character of what was later to be built and known as the University Research Library. Paul Miles succeeded Williams, as Williams did Harlow, as the library building planning czar. A growing library needs someone on its staff who can use a slide rule and has three-dimensional sight. I was deficient in both.

I have recounted these moves in detail, for they were the reasons for the success of library development at UCLA. My philosophy of personnel administration was part of my native equipment, inherited from my father. I took no courses, read no books, or had any experience in personnel work prior to 1944. What I did have was the power to perceive character and motivation, whereby I knew without being told, as when I saw Vosper's picture and knew that he was part of my destiny. I was motivated by the need to have librarians who could do what I couldn't do, or could do it better, which was most everything relating to the operation of a library. I knew people and I knew books, and I loved them both with an intensity approaching passion. This was my own, and I tirelessly did the things that brought books and people together. It was knowing my limitations and my strengths and acting accordingly. It is true that I became known best as a bookman, but the record shows that I was also successful as an administrator.

I selected able people, then I gave them authority, encouragement, praise, and public recognition. I took credit for nothing that I did not do myself. And that is all I have to say about library administration.

As a result of this policy, many of my staff, in addition to those mentioned, went on to responsible positions throughout the land.

Regent Dickson had been pushing for a library school at UCLA ever since 1930, when for economy reasons City Librarian Everett T. Perry wanted the Los Angeles Public Library's school transferred to UCLA. Goodwin and Mitchell were against it. The time was not ripe. Berkeley had to weather the Depression. UCLA needed to develop a major library; and so in 1936 the LAPL school went to the University of Southern California, UCLA's crosstown rival.

Soon after I took office in 1944, Regent Dickson came to see me about "that school of the library." I asked for time. I promised to get to it, and I did. I did not know then that it would take fifteen years of fighting. That is the story that ends this book.

Although it was most unlikely, Goodwin and I were reconciled. Upon Dean Mitchell's retirement in 1947, I persuaded my alma mater, Occidental, to award him an honorary LL.D., and when he came down for the ceremony, I gave a luncheon in his honor, to which were invited President Sproul, Provost Dykstra, Professor Westergaard, Professor Dunn, actor–book collector Jean Hersholt–and Goodwin. Mitchell predicted that he wouldn't refuse–and he didn't.

When Goodwin arrived, Mitchell said, "Howdy, Jack, it's good of you to come." It was good of him and I made every effort to please him, the climax coming after lunch, when I escorted Goodwin through the nearly finished new wing. It was his first visit to the library since the day he left, three years before, and his gentle face was happy as he inspected every detail of the new unit.

He did not live long after that. The next time I saw him, he was in his coffin. In my final year as Dean of the Library School I persuaded Linda West, one of the best students I ever had, to undertake a professional biography of John Edward Goodwin. Without the foundation he laid, I could never have reared the structure Vosper is pushing even higher, and without the initial appointment he gave me, I would never have had a life at UCLA. And so I write gratefully in his memory.

BOOKS ARE BASIC

People, librarians no exception, are forgotten. Books remain. Long after I am forgotten as man and librarian, the books I collected for UCLA will, barring cataclysm, be there in the Clark and on campus, awaiting the touch of hand, the sight of eye that brings them to life. It may be that some of them will have a long wait before they are found by a curious or needful reader. I used to roam through the stacks, taking books from the shelves at random, always thrilled when I was the first to charge out a volume since it had been acquired many years before.

From the first, my collecting for the UCLA libraries was not geared to immediate needs, although there was steady buying with them in mind. I was seeking also to amass materials for scholars to come, to give to the library in a short generation the maturity acquired over the years by older institutions. To a native passion for books, I brought the experience gained at Vroman's and Zeitlin's and during my apprenticeship in the library, so that I knew what the library needed and how to go about getting it.

Only one thing was lacking: money. This was not true at the Clark. There the endowment yielded a steady income, although I had trouble in getting the canny Sproul to give me complete information on the budget to which I was entitled as Director. Not until bookman Franklin Murphy came as Chancellor did I get both information and dollars in abundance.

The main library budget was shamefully inadequate, cut, as I have noted, to $55,000, from which everything, including periodical subscriptions, had to be bought. I soon asked the President for more. The opportunity came when Ernest Dawson, dean of Los Angeles' antiquarian booksellers, offered us the Olive Percival Collection of 19th-century English and American children's books for $1,000.

It was my habit to go to the Clark Library each Wednesday to review matters with Archer, then proceed to the University Club for the weekly luncheon at the Zamorano Club's round table, adjourning afterward to Dawson's Book Shop around the corner. The city has never known another like Father Dawson, a little fireball of a man, who bought and sold books in lots large and small. Fast turnover was his method; and it paid a librarian to make regular visits to the shop, for the books came and went fast.

Olive Percival, a spinster insurance agent and collector of books and art, had died in 1945, leaving so many treasures that it took Louis Samuels two weeks to inventory the contents of her home in the Arroyo Seco. Dawson bought her library of 10,000 volumes, including the juveniles, and had yet to move the books to his shop. When he offered the juveniles sight unseen, saying that he wanted UCLA, his son Glen's alma mater, to have first refusal, I did not refuse. I said yes, and arranged to take delivery the following Wednesday. Father Dawson's word that they were choice was all that was needed.

On entering the shop a week later, I was greeted by Dawson, a telegram in his hand. It was from Dr. Rosenbach in Philadelphia. "Offer $3,000 Percival juveniles."

"Do you mean our deal's off?"

"I do not," was Father's reply. "I just wanted you to know what a bargain you're getting."

He was right. It was a bargain. The Percival juveniles formed the base on which we built UCLA's now large and distinguished collection of children's books.

I still owed Dawson the $1,000. Upon seeing Sproul I apologized for begging.

"If you don't ask, who will?" he said. "Are they worth it?"

I told him of the Rosenbach telegram. He was impressed.

"I'll give you half. Take the other half from your budget."

"What budget?" I said to myself, as I made a quick exit.

So I went to the Library Committee for the $500. They required supporting letters from the several academic departments to which early children's books would have research interest. I induced English, Folklore, and Education to support the request.

It was a time-consuming procedure, and if I had kept booksellers waiting for decisions, I would have lost many good buys. When I wanted something for sure, I gave a firm order, took possession of the books, then set about getting approval and finding the money.

I learned this the hard way, by letting a prize get away because I failed to act promptly.

It was a set of the Oriental Translation Fund publications, a Victorian project of translating, with original texts also present, of Chinese, Japanese, Turkish, Persian, Arabian, and Sanskrit classics, a noble set in full morocco, bearing the gilt arms of the Duke of Rutland. The hundred or more folio volumes were priced absurdly low at $900. I hesitated giving Dawson a firm order, for at that time UCLA had no instruction or research in any of the Oriental or Slavic languages. In view of the limited budget, I knew that the Library Committee would begrudge money for books whose use lay in the unforeseeable future.

Oh, for a crystal ball! It was not many years before UCLA launched major programs in every one of those Oriental languages, and Slavic too. So I told Father Dawson I would let him know later. I awoke the next morning, determined to buy the set and pay for it somehow, perhaps by wrapping packages in my spare time. I phoned him as soon as I reached the library.

"I'm sorry," he said. "It was sold not long after you left."

"Who bought it?"

"Dr. Von Kleinsmid."

And so the set went to USC, whose bibliophilic Chancellor roamed the city, snapping up bargains such as this. Before his retirement as Provost, UCLA's Ernest Carroll Moore had done likewise, and it was his bookish leadership in the 1920's, more than Goodwin's or the faculty's, that had brought the library several great collections en bloc, such as the Fiske, Cowan, Kluge, Chuquet, and Dickey.

An exception on the faculty was Professor Gustave O. Arlt, a young Germanic scholar who had persuaded Goodwin and the Library Committee to buy several Germanic collections—the Hoffman, Burdach, Bremer, and Dahlerup, all formed by professors, the acquisition of which gave UCLA strength in 18th-, 19th- and 20th-century literature and linguistics. Arlt had annoyed

Goodwin by an article, co-authored with John J. Lund, the philologist-librarian whose leaving for Duke University Library opened the place I filled in 1938. The article, which appeared in the *Library Journal* in 1937, was critical of the kind of library organization found at UCLA. It was a good article, but it did not succeed in changing anything at UCLA under Goodwin.

Arlt later became Dean of the Graduate Division at the time the Library School was created, and as one of the late Regent Dickson's closest friends, it was fitting that Arlt share the platform with Paul Horgan when we dedicated the school. Arlt was one of the few faculty members who worked at my compulsive tempo. Most of them were too deliberate. The reason that I was able to accomplish what I did at UCLA is that I was responsible to the Chancellor or President. Whenever the faculty had responsibility, as in the case of the book budget, delays occurred. The later Murphy-Vosper axis succeeded in virtually eliminating the faculty from even book fund authority.

Vosper kept adroitly extending faculty confidence in our buying, and we obtained more and more free money. He and Professor Charles L. Mowat increased our British Empire and local history materials. With Professor Wayland D. Hand, the library embarked on a folklore collecting program which eventually ranked UCLA with Indiana as the country's major collections. Professors Majl Ewing and Hugh Dick in English, Francis Crowley in French, Marion Zeitlin in Spanish and Portuguese, Clifford Zierer in geography, Cordell Durrell in geology, Gordon Ball in zoology, and Max Dunn in chemistry were also diligent and skillful book selectors. Vosper and I ranged the local antiquarian shops, buying anything that promised research use, no matter how far off.

One day in a Hollywood bookstore I saw on the floor

several hundred volumes on a single subject: roulette—a collection in French and German on every aspect of the game. The price of $45 was a giveaway. I paid for them with my personal check—the owner needed instant cash —loaded them in my car and took them to the library.

For years the collection remained untouched on the shelves, classified under GV—Games, Sports, Pastimes; and with only an occasional twinge of conscience I would see it as I passed through the stacks. And then one day the shelves were empty. I rushed to the loan file and found every book charged out to the United States Navy's Campus Institute of Numerical Analysis!

In addition to Ernest Dawson and later his sons Glen and Muir, the library benefitted by offerings from Jake Zeitlin and other local dealers. On trips to Chicago and New York I bought cheaply items which today would cost in the thousands, namely the first books of Yeats, Joyce, Pound, and Hemingway. I also bought for $200 the correspondence of D. H. Lawrence with Pino Orioli, the publisher of *Lady Chatterley's Lover*. Time and again book trade experience proved rewarding. By knowledge of and sympathy with bookdealers, I gained their confidence and first offers of material. By speaking and travelling and writing, I became a liaison between libraries and bookstores. We also made the UCLA library a repository for booksellers' archives. After Ernest Dawson's death, we established an endowment fund to buy books about books in his memory; and from his sons and daughter we received the firm's business records. Holmes, Epstein, and Zeitlin of Los Angeles and Ellis of London also placed their archives at UCLA. A student book collecting prize contest was established by Robert B. Campbell, pioneer UCLA bookseller. This practice of encouraging intellectual intercourse between the library and booksellers has been vigorously furthered by Robert Vosper.

The forties were a time of gathering momentum, experience, and funds; then in the fifties I made two major book coups, the Michael Sadleir and the C. K. Ogden collections. The first was a collaboration between Vosper, me and Professor Bradford A. Booth, and booksellers John Carter, Dudley Massey, and David A. Randall. I should include also Provost Gordon N. Ray of Illinois who almost snatched away from UCLA the peerless collection of Victorian fiction; for at last, unable to raise the necessary $65,000, Ray magnanimously threw his not inconsiderable weight behind UCLA's effort.

This acquisition involved several years of correspondence—some would call it intrigue—and London visits to Sadleir by Booth and me, before Sproul came through in a photo finish that nipped Illinois at the tape and gave us the Sadleir collection as a Christmas present. The irreplaceable library of yellowbacks and three-deckers, all in the pristine condition Sadleir insisted on, became a magnet, drawing scholars and bookmen to UCLA from all over the world.

When after the war the scholarly bookseller John Carter was serving as the British Ambassador's personal secretary, he alerted us that he and Sir Roger Makins would be in Los Angeles and that he wanted especially for Sir Roger to see the Sadleir collection. "Phone the British Consul," Carter wrote, "and find out what local plans he has made." When I did so and reported that Sir Roger would be wanting to see the novels, I got a bureaucratic brush-off from an underling.

Not for long. An hour later the Consul General himself phoned to apologize. He had heard from Sir Roger. When would be a convenient time? And so a few days later Carter brought the tall ambassador and Lady Makins for books and for lunch. I shall never forget the delight with which they handled the rare volumes, all the while the urbane John Carter purred and winked.

As well as a great bookman, John Carter is an elegant ballroom dancer. We have no ballroom in our Malibu home, but the smooth cement patio is a good dance floor; and one time when Carter was our house guest, he and Fay danced divinely, just the two of them, for an hour or more, to the music provided by me on our Steinway grand—the same piano on which, years before, I had played the tango for Fay's aunt.

I have told other stories in earlier books. "To Newbury to Buy an Old Book" was an account of acquiring the Harmsworth Collection of 17th-century English Protestant theology for the Clark Library, and "Rendezvous in Cadogan Square" recalled the C. K. Ogden purchase for $100,000 of 70,000 volumes on myriad subjects which was divided among the several campuses of the university. It was here that the Library Council served as the instrument which persuaded the President to provide the funds; and as the secretary that year of 1957, Donald Coney gave strong and unfailing support in the negotiations which were carried on by me in London.

The Isaac Foot collection came after I had become Dean of the Library School, but it was because of an earlier contact with Foot that his library was offered and referred by me to the Library Council. It was Secretary Edwin T. Coman of the Riverside campus who went to London and Plymouth and negotiated for the $150,000 purchase, and it was Librarian Donald C. Davidson and his staff of the Santa Barbara campus who effectively distributed the books statewide. When Cy Silver, one of the staff who worked on this project came as a library school student, he prepared and published a paper on the acquisition and distribution of the Ogden and Foot libraries. Foot had some author and subject collections that were more comprehensive than anything in Ogden's libraries; for example, Bibles and Commonwealth tracts, the latter incidentally enriching the Clark's holdings by several thousand items; but for variety and examples of the best books on nearly every subject in the encyclopedia, Ogden's library was the most erudite and interesting. And of course on the subject of Basic English, it was peerless.

Fortune's way of entering and reentering a man's life was never better illustrated by the manner in which my life and Foot's touched and drew apart, with results not apparent until nearly twenty years later.

It happened on that fateful trip to Chicago when I went back to be interviewed at Northwestern. On the return, the final hour out of Pasadena, I heard a commotion in the next roomette, and upon investigating found an elderly Englishman trying to close suitcases into which he had overpacked a number of books.

"If you will pardon me," I said, "I'll do it for you so that they will close."

And I did, drawing on my experience as a shipping clerk.

He had five suitcases of books and one of clothes, and he proved to be the Honorable Isaac Foot, Lord Mayor of Plymouth, travelling for the British government on a wartime mission.

"There are some people in Southern California I must see," Foot told me when I had his bags ready and we were chatting as the *Super Chief* rolled down the home stretch, "but there's only one I want to see. I don't suppose he's still alive. He would be a very old man. I don't suppose you'd know. He is the authority on Drake. His name is Henry R. Wagner.

To Foot's astonishment I did know, even to Wagner's telephone number, and I arranged a day or two later to pick up Foot at the Biltmore Hotel and drive him to San

127

Marino to call on Henry Wagner, then eighty-two years old, and left them to talk Drake and books.

When Isaac Foot died years later, a note was found in his desk, suggesting if the library were sold, that his sons, the many noted "Feet," get in touch with a librarian at UCLA, a man who knew how to pack books. It recalled Professor Grant's terse comment after the Westergaard committee had me before them, "He can carry his weight in books."

There is the explanation of why throughout my career as librarian and teacher, I constantly held up to beginners the importance (and the rewards) of physical contact with books. And the joy of handling them. I remember once when Bill Jackson visited the Clark after I had become Director, and I watched him go along the shelves, taking volume after volume into his hands, opening, glancing, then putting them back, all done swiftly with ease and grace. "Once handled, never forgotten" was his only comment—gospel words of the greatest bookman of our time.

SOME WRITERS AND THEIR PAPERS

Libraries and literature, literature and libraries. How can they be separated? I went as a child to the library for books to read, for tales that took me out of myself and far away. "I should like to rise and go, where the golden apples grow." I did rise, did go, and because of books. I loved Nellie Keith and Althea Warren because they were bookish yea-sayers. I became a librarian I suppose, thinking back on it, because it seemed a way to come closer to books, to literature, and then to bring others with me, to lead, to share. "Everyman, I will go with thee by thy side, in thy most need be thy guide."

From the beginning of my studies and my career, it never occurred to me not to associate libraries and literature, not only of the past but of the present as well. Thus the very first library exhibits I arranged, while still a student, were of a living writer's, a living printer's works: Robinson Jeffers and Ward Ritchie. And the collections I formed of their books I naturally placed in libraries where they would be preserved and serve others, Jeffers at Occidental College, Ritchie in the Clark

Library. The books of the next two writers I collected
with zeal, John Steinbeck and D. H. Lawrence, I finally
parted with to Harvard and UCLA respectively. A
librarian who does not collect books personally is a poor
thing indeed, and furthermore I deem it immoral to
retain possession of books one no longer reads frequently. I must say too that my passion for Steinbeck's
writing did not continue after *The Grapes of Wrath*. It
seemed to me that he reached zenith in that epic of the
Okies. I believed likewise about Hemingway and *For
Whom the Bell Tolls*.

I enjoyed friendship with Aldous Huxley from 1937,
when he introduced my catalog of Lawrence's manuscripts, until his death in 1962. Through the good offices
of Jake Zeitlin, we had arranged for UCLA to receive
Huxley's manuscripts. We procrastinated in making the
transfer from his Hollywood home. Fire destroyed them
all. We did receive Zeitlin's collection of the manuscripts
and letters given to him earlier by Huxley; and after
Huxley's death, the library issued a catalog of them
compiled by George Wickes; and in the Library School
we held a memorial meeting, addressed by Zeitlin,
Robert Kirsch, and myself.

The culmination of this series of public exhibitions at
UCLA, 1938–43, was one of Huxley's books and manuscripts, for which I also compiled a checklist, and which
was opened with a lecture on campus by the writer.
Again, I had the privilege of introducing him.

We first met Frieda Lawrence in 1941 when, on our
return from Cambridge, Fay and I visited her on the
ranch above Taos, and later when she wintered in Los
Angeles. Then Professor Ewing and I arranged a
campus program in memory of Lawrence, at which
Huxley and Frieda spoke. She was a tremendous sight,
striding down the aisle in her peasant costume, to the
jingle of Navajo jewelry. She was abundantly alive,

though deferring always to Huxley's tall, keen, pensive presence.

Upon reading through the files after succeeding Goodwin, I came upon a letter to him from the Librarian of Congress, Luther H. Evans, introducing Richard Aldington, who would appreciate receiving library privileges. Here was another of the Lawrence group, whose books on Lawrence, and his early Imagist poetry, and above all his novels *Death of a Hero* and *All Men Are Enemies*, had given me pleasure. I wrote at once to his Hollywood address, asking that he come in the office next time he was at the library. We became fast friends, as did his wife Netta and Fay, their daughter Catha and our sons, Norman and Wilkie; and I set to work in assembling an Aldington collection in the library, to which he gave many volumes of his books translated into other languages. After the war he returned to France. Fay and I were to visit him near Bourges on our trip in 1963. Death arrived before we did. In London in 1951, Netta Aldington painted oil portraits of Fay and me, and our friendship with her has continued.

The German cultural refugee colony in Los Angeles included Thomas Mann, Lion Feuchtwanger, Franz Werfel, and Arnold Schoenberg. Professor Arlt was in touch with them. When Werfel died, Arlt induced his widow, Alma Mahler Werfel, to give his literary papers to UCLA. Feuchtwanger's research library we could have had as a gift if we had been willing to administer it in the widow's home as a branch library. We were content to let USC have this responsibility. Thomas Mann's papers went to Yale. Schoenberg's manuscripts were promised to UCLA, but the composer changed his mind when, upon retirement from the UCLA faculty, he was shocked by the smallness of his pension. Henry Schnitzler, son of Arthur Schnitzler, the Viennese doctor-writer, was a member of UCLA's Theater Arts faculty. He gave the Library his father's journals, millions of words written in an almost illegible hand. Their eventual publication will be of importance in Austrian literary history.

I was alert for writers using the UCLA Library and always made extra efforts to serve them, believing that the use of a great collection of books should be unlimited. I regarded UCLA as a depot for all who were drawn by its magnetic resources and we were constantly mailing books around the West to writers: Kenneth Rexroth in San Francisco, Henry Miller in Big Sur, Haniel Long in Santa Fe, Duncan Brent in Escondido, and to a fire watcher named Scott Greer on an Oregon mountain top. Irving Stone, Guy Endore, Harold Lamb, and Robert Payne were writers I befriended by serving their needs, and all four made the UCLA Library the repository for their manuscripts.

I cannot say that I became friends with Dylan Thomas. Except for the inspired campus reading he gave in 1950, he was drunk throughout his stay. We made a recording of his reading, a passionate memorial of his visit, and after the Library School opened, we played it each year for the students.

This activity of reading, collecting, friendship and sharing, I regarded as central, not peripheral, to librarianship, and I employed every opportunity to speak out against those who viewed and practiced librarianship as a technical process.

The conversion of William Everson to Roman Catholicism, whereby he became Brother Antoninus, affected our friendship. Our earlier correspondence forms a rich record of our growth. Afterward we limited ourselves to occasional meetings. My belief in his genius never waned, however, as I watched him become a latter-day Hopkins. His manuscripts as a poet and his work as a printer we amassed in the Clark Library, as well as his taped readings on campuses throughout the country.

It was through enjoyment of his poetry that I was led to friendship with Kenneth Rexroth; and the subsequent collection of his papers in the UCLA Library is of major importance in the literature of our time. Denied service by the Berkeley Library and finding the San Francisco Public Library's collection inadequate, Rexroth depended upon UCLA for his needs in many fields.

Another major collection formed was that of Henry Miller. Our friendship deepened with the years. I wrote of it in my foreword to the paperback *Intimate Henry Miller*. I championed his work when it was still forbidden in the United States, and when it was finally published and brought into court, I was the first witness for the defense at the Los Angeles trial of the bookseller who sold *Tropic of Cancer*.

Although both prosecutor and judge gave me a bad time, I found it a lively experience. The former began by asking me to read aloud one of the coarser passages. In objecting I offered to read the entire book aloud, saying that it could not be judged piecemeal. Then he asked me to translate a French poem sung by the students at the lycée in Dijon. "It is not by Miller," I said. "He is merely quoting it. I believe it is by Blaise Cendrars, a well-known man of letters." The judge cut me off. The prosecutor kept concentrating on scatology and sex, and I kept insisting that the book is important as a social document and should be judged as a whole. I asked if I might read aloud the transcendent description of a winter night in Dijon, that I had lived there and recognized the poetic fidelity of the passage. My request was denied.

Then the prosecutor sought to discredit my authority as a critic because I was a personal friend of Miller, saying that I had gone so far as to deliver library books in person to Miller, as if that were the ultimate crime. Furthermore, he said, Dr. Powell has had a book by Miller actually dedicated to him. With that I was dismissed from the stand.

The trial ended with the bookseller's conviction, although it was later reversed by a higher court. It was not long before Miller's works were sold openly throughout the land. Alongside the flood of "hard-core" pornography, they had become curiously old-fashioned. The last of the Victorians, I called Miller, in a Phi Beta Kappa address given on the Riverside campus of the university.

During Miller's residence in Big Sur, before beatniks had swarmed down the coast and driven him away, I paid many visits to his eyrie on Partington Ridge. We would bathe at the Hot Springs, and then I would play on the upright piano in the lounge, while Miller would hum along off-key.

Andy Horn was with me on one of those visits to Miller, and had brought along a tape recorder. After dinner at the Hot Springs, I sat down at the piano and didn't stop playing until long after midnight, now accompaniments, now solo. People drifted in and out, singing and dancing. Wynn Bullock, the photographer and an old South Pasadenan, recalled his years as an opera singer, as I accompanied his sweet tenor. Big Ralph Gilman's mother, a chesty contralto, sang *Harvest Moon* until the roof bulged. Judy Brandt, sultry wife of the Carmel Valley postmaster, danced a tango. Beer flowed as Gilman threw open the Lodge's icebox. Through it all I kept on playing, utterly relaxed and happy. And through it all Andy kept the tape recorder going. I still have the tapes. *Quelle nuit!*

Gerhart Münch, the concert pianist, lived near Miller. His passion was for Scriabin, and once after Miller and I had heard Münch play the Russian composer's sonatas for hour after hour, I was moved to invite Münch to give an all-Scriabin recital at UCLA. It took place on a warm July evening, the hall filled with our friends and the local Teuton colony led by the German consul, not to speak of assorted Russians. It was a triumph, and we have a tape recording, made by Andrew Horn, to recall it.

I cite this as an example of the fecundating influence of Miller on those who came within his orbit. He is a rare and wonderful man, as well as a powerful writer. All that I did benefitted from his friendship.

It was Lawrence Durrell's poetry that first led me to read and collect him, long before the *Alexandria Quartet* made him world famous and before I knew that he and Henry Miller were old friends. I met Durrell only once, fifteen years after I began to collect his books and after intermittent correspondence. Then it was by chance, at the Dome in Montparnasse, when we were seated in adjoining booths. I recognized him straightway, introduced myself as "the other Larry," and received a Durrellesque bear hug. He is a great gay person.

When Miller began to give the library his letters from Durrell, it was apparent that a selection of their correspondence would make a great book. Miller agreed. Durrell shied away from the idea. It was not until the young scholar, George Wickes, came my way, engaged in writing a profile of Aldous Huxley for the *Paris Review*, that the ideal editor was found for the project. Wickes went to France and succeeded in obtaining Durrell's blessing. The published volume was a great success.

Together with Alan Thomas of Bournemouth, the antiquarian bookseller and Durrell's oldest friend, I contributed a Durrell checklist to *The Book Collector*. This was expanded into a full-scale bibliography by Brooke

Whiting and Robert Potter, and published by the UCLA Library upon occasion of the gift of my Durrell collection in honor of Robert Vosper's succeeding me as University Librarian.

These were bibliographical projects in which literature and librarianship were wedded. These authors' books I enjoyed, as well as holding the men personally in great affection. I never limited my library collecting to personal enthusiasms, however, and a mere listing of the research materials gathered by librarians and faculty would be a very long list indeed, to which I plan to devote another book.

The literary history of our time can be written with more understanding because of the archival collections at UCLA. No other Western library paid such attention to living writers.

As my personal library kept growing beyond our capacity to shelve it, I made steady donations to the Occidental Library. Once my books were collected, read, and absorbed, my interest in owning them waned, and thus my alma mater eventually received my collections of Henry Miller, Everson-Antoninus, Llewelyn Powys, H. J. Massingham, and Robinson Jeffers. Most of my Western Americana review copies went to the college, as did my mother's books upon her death, including a numerous Samuel Pepys collection.

SPEAKING OF BOOKS

It seems to me important to give some account of my public speaking, for it became a means of making friends (and enemies) and of influencing people to read and to embrace librarianship. For twenty years I went about the land like Johnny Appleseed, scattering books (and prejudices), and inducing new growth. Eventually I spoke in most of the United States, in Europe and Asia. The total number of talks surely ran into the hundreds, even to a thousand or more.

Once I had learned how to prepare and deliver a talk—and the only test of a talk is that people sit still and listen—it seemed to listeners an easy, natural thing for me to do. It wasn't, at least not in the beginning. Learning how was long and hard. As birthright I had qualities of personality, energy, and a compulsion for self-expression; and yet I was panic-stricken when I had to appear before an audience, either in boyhood piano recitals or as yell leader in high school. I had to force myself to go on stage and to keep from running away. Orchestra work, dramatics, and debating gradually helped me to gain ease in front of large groups. I suppose it was a desire for recognition and applause that brought me through those terrors of stage fright.

Extemporaneous speaking was hard because of an inability to assemble my diffused thoughts. My timing was bad. I didn't know how to end. Then I would panic and say outrageous things, as once at Occidental College, long after graduation, when President Bird asked me to speak to a student assembly about Lawrence, at the time of a campus production of his play *David*. I got off track and denounced Presbyterianism, students who studied economics and business instead of literature, and people's failure to recognize Lawrence in his lifetime. The reason was that I had not prepared my remarks. I still remember President Bird's chiding as he saw me to my car.

"Larry, do you really dislike us as much as that?"

"You know I love you and the college too."

"Then for the blessed Lord's sake, why didn't you say so?"

From that fiasco I learned to jot notes on a card before speaking extemporaneously and never to rise without knowing the main points I planned to make.

Why did I offend so many people in the library world in the course of my speaking and writing? As I see it, it was because of a personal, autobiographical, egocentric, didactic, flamboyant, hyperbolic manner. My first deep stirring of the animals came after an article contributed to the *Stechert-Hafner Book News* called "The Chief Librarian, Bookman or Administrator." It provoked Maurice Tauber to reply, and this in turn led to correspondence on both sides. Our points of view were hopelessly divergent.

In reviewing *The Alchemy of Books*, a New England librarian called it "intensely personal," as though this were one of the deadly sins. If I had replied, I would have held up Emerson as a model I had striven to emulate. Emerson's essays all came from his journals and public addresses. I regard him, with Franklin and Jefferson, as one of our greatest Americans.

After keynoting the ALA conference at New York in 1952, with the address called "The Alchemy of Books," I found myself in the Waldorf elevator with a New England university librarian and some of his junior staff. The older man gave me a pained smile as we rode up, floor after floor, in utter silence. ". . . and never the twain shall meet."

A more forthright reaction came afterward from Ralph Shaw, the most creative of all library housekeepers. He rushed down the aisle to the platform and handed me a specially printed card which read, "I sure liked that load of b——t."

All through that talk I remarked a little old woman in the front row who never took her eyes off me. She wore a heavy coat and a felt hat pulled down close to her face. I met her afterward. She was Anne Carroll Moore, the greatest of children's librarians. She too was a New Englander, not given to many words. Those she used pleased me. "I like what you said."

What I kept saying, in talk after talk, was that as custodians of the world's literature, librarians should be the best-read of all people, and that if we wished to rise in public esteem higher than housekeepers and technicians, we should stop talking and behaving like such when we appeared in public. I sought to create a public image of librarians as cultural agents. These things were said without moderation, and I charged the library schools in particular with fostering dullness.

After a talk at the ALA Far Western Regional conference at Vancouver in 1949, I was called by an ALA official a "sentimental scholar," and I believe he meant it in a pejorative sense. Something far worse nearly happened to me at that meeting: it was the first time I had spoken with new dentures, and at one point I nearly lost 'em.

After "The Gift to Be Simple" at the South Carolina Library Association conference in Clemson, I was called a "biblio-simpleton." My use of hyperbole led people to take me literally and to write irate letters to the journals.

At the Detroit conference in 1965, which I keynoted with "Great Land of Libraries," I looked down on the press table directly below the platform. There sat Eric Moon, making notes for the unflattering report that appeared later in the *Library Journal*. John Berry was holding his ears against the reverberations in the vastness of the convention hall. Sol Malkin was smoking a cigar and sipping brandy and grinning like the Buddha. Those three were all I needed for audience.

So many of my "enemies" were humorless, as the ALA official who castigated me when, in the *New York Times Book Review*, I called several of our leading librarians without library school training "mavericks." With earnest piety he leaped to their defense, not realizing I had meant to compliment them.

My best talks came when the time, the place, and the occasion produced a sense of certainty and power in my preparation and delivery. Before such times I worked on draft after draft, cutting and tightening, so that when it came time to give the talk, I had it all but memorized. I learned to speak as though without a manuscript. By employing things I had learned in college dramatics about timing, pauses, silences, and contrasts, I was able to reach out and hold people. Some did not like my theatrical style any more than what I said, but they did hear me out. I was never picketed.

In the autumn of 1953, I went to Ann Arbor to give the annual Randolph G. Adams Memorial Lecture. I had not seen him again after that one meeting at UCLA, fifteen years earlier. Once I almost made it, but the plane was grounded by fog at La Guardia Field and the flight to Detroit was cancelled. Now Adams was dead and I was in the William L. Clements Library he had directed with great brilliance. The oak-panelled drawing room gleamed with subdued lights. People were dressed formally. President Harlan Hatcher introduced me, and I was glad to have prepared "Three Loves Have I" to the best of my ability.

It was a talk about books, of course, their collecting, reading, and being given away to libraries. As I spoke, with increasing intensity, I felt Randolph Adams at my side. It was a strange experience, as I sought to infuse my words with gratitude for what he had done for me in those lean years of my apprenticeship. His widow wrote me afterward that she too had strongly sensed his presence.

Publication of that lecture in *A Passion for Books* brought a visitor to my office; an elderly little woman not over five feet tall, wearing a smart tweed suit and a saucy hat. She was Rachel Hunt of Pittsburgh, known in the book world as the greatest collector of illustrated botanical works. Her husband, Roy Hunt, was president of the Aluminum Corporation of America.

"My husband and I are giving Carnegie Tech a new library building," she explained her call, "a penthouse on which will house my collection. May I get some ideas from your Clark Library?"

We drove straightway to West Adams.

That meeting led to my being asked by Rachel and Roy Hunt to speak at the dedication of their library. It was a gala affair, assembling the aristocracy of the book world: John Carter, Wilmarth Lewis, Fred Adams, Bill Jackson, Curt Buhler, John Gordan, Philip Hofer, Waller Barrett, Lynton Massey, John Cook Wyllie,

Lawrence Wroth, Donald and Mary Hyde, Fred Goff, and of course, Sol Malkin. The academic procession was piped in by a squealing ensemble of pipers, and the hood of my honorary degree was lined with the Carnegie tartan. My talk was called "Building, with Books."

In 1957 I was invited to give the British Library Association's Annual Lecture at their conference in Harrogate. We flew to London via the Arctic Circle and Copenhagen, then drove a new Jaguar 3.4 north on A1, stopping in Lincoln and York to see the cathedrals. Formal dress (mine hired from Moss Bros.), the blood-red decor of the municipal opera house, and an un-orthodox introduction by Jacob Bronowski, the cele-brated brain-truster president of the L.A., all heightened the excitement I felt in giving "Books Will Be Read," the latest of my broadsides into the ranks of the library philistines.

I began by reading "Travel" from *A Child's Garden of Verses*, declaring that it was that poem above all else that had made me "rise and go," bringing me this time from the farthest southwest of the United States to the West Riding of Yorkshire, just over Hadrian's Wall from the land that bore R. L. S. Bronowski entered into the liveliness of my ensuing remarks by rising at one point, after I had successfully tossed off a tongue-twist-ing sentence, to pour a glass of water and hand it to me with a bow. The audience cheered.

Backstage afterward I was approached by a group of older men who introduced themselves as Lancashire town library councillors.

"If thee isn't Quaker," one of them said, "thee surely speaks as one."

"I am indeed a birthright Quaker," I said, and we embraced in what some Englishmen, from farther south in the land, might have called a shocking display of feeling.

Occasions like those compensated for the wear and tear of travelling.

Both were considerable on the two speaking trips I made to Japan, each time upon invitation of Mary J. Carter, the petite, red-haired, green-eyed Command Librarian of the Pacific Air Force. She had entered library work through the UCLA reserve book room under Deborah King. I took part in conferences of armed forces librarians from throughout the Pacific theater. Theirs was library service far removed from the campus. It was dependent upon books, and it was about books and reading that we spoke, I to them, they to me.

In Tokyo I was hosted by Ruth Sieben-Morgen and Tony Dakan, two dedicated air force librarians, and by Naomi Fukuda and Yushio Fujino of the International House Library and by my colleagues on the faculty of the Japan Library School at Keio University.

I went each time alone to the sombre Imperial Hotel, and musing there over tea and toast, I imagined what my life would have been had I jumped ship on my first visit to Japan in 1925 as musician aboard the *President Harrison*, and become a very much lesser Lafcadio Hearn.

In all those years of travel and talks and the dedication of several library buildings, I gave only one commencement address, at the University of Arizona in 1961. I was determined not to bore the graduates, as I had been bored at many a commencement by platitudinous moralizing. I called the talk "The Little Package," by which I meant The Book, and I sought to make it a kind of time bomb, set to explode a decade hence, when the graduates would have mostly become middle-aged readers of nothing but magazines.

In preparing the talk I did not know that seated next to me on the platform would be a candidate for an honorary degree, America's most influential magazine publisher, Henry Luce. After the talk, delivered in the open air under the desert stars, Luce gave me a wry smile and a limp hand. His wife, Clare Booth Luce, gave me more. "I liked it," she said.

So did the graduates and their parents, from whom I had many letters. And I made lasting friends of President Richard A. Harvill and his wife George, a former librarian.

Of all the many talks I gave, none was more lastingly influential than one about *Islandia*, Austin Wright's utopian novel. I called it "All That Is Poetic in Life," and gave it many times throughout the land. In it I deplored publishers' having let it go out of print. This talk and the ensuing letters from auditors finally led them to reprint *Islandia*, first hardbound, then in paperback. It led also to friendship with Wright's brother, his daughters and one son, to correspondence with scores of "Islandians," and to Wright's papers being deposited at Harvard in the Houghton Library under Bill Jackson's care.

Born with a thick skin that thickened as I grew older, I never brooded over the unfavorable things said and written about me, nor did I attempt to strike back. On the contrary, it pleased me to find good to say about my severest critics. About Jesse Shera, for example, whose review of *A Passion for Books* would have driven a sensitive man to a breakdown. Expecting me to blast Shera, Eric Moon wickedly sent me one of Shera's books for review. Instead I praised it. This temporarily mollified the caustic Buckeye, and he went so far as to speak well of me in his column. Once.

What I said and wrote about librarianship was not calculated either to please or displease auditors and readers. It was simply my way of expressing myself, of attracting attention, of holding the limelight; and it was excellent preparation for my final years as a teacher. When the time came to lead students into library service,

I had something to say and knew how to say it. On my travels I had met every kind of librarian in their home libraries. I knew about the Bodleian Library in Oxford and the Box Car Library in Ash Fork, and that a catalysis of reader and book occurred in both. I came to teaching, after fifty-four years of preparation, with a bagful of experience.

THE ORGANIZATION MAN

I was a good organization man in my time. Although critical of professional groups, I never broke with them. Unlike Randolph Adams, who from outside the ALA kept lobbing charges over the wall, I made myself an inside nuisance to some, a conscience voice to others. However bad one's aim, he couldn't miss hitting the elephantine ALA somewhere in its anatomy. I was a joiner from the beginning, close on target, and after I became an administrator I encouraged my staff to join. Whatever its shortcomings as a bureaucracy, the ALA was indispensable to our lowly status as professionals.

At the ALA Conference at San Francisco in 1939, President Milton Ferguson and Executive Secretary Carl Milam attacked President Roosevelt's nomination of Archibald MacLeish as Librarian of Congress. Their printed protest was circulated, giving reasons why a librarian, rather than a literary man, should occupy the profession's highest post. I was careful to save two copies, one for my literary, one for my library collection.

I have already noted how Randolph Adams encouraged me from his office in the Clements to support MacLeish and that Jens Nyholm and I also joined in this cause. I was unknown in the profession when I rose at a general session and seconded Nyholm's remarks on behalf of MacLeish. We, and a few others whose applause made them conspicuous, believed (and time proved us right) that MacLeish would be an inspired spokesman for the rapprochement of librarianship and literature. After I sat down, Mitchell caught my eye and although he wagged his finger, he was smiling.

When I took office in 1944, Althea Warren was the president of the ALA. She phoned one day and asked if she and Carl Milam could call. I realized later that it was to give the Executive Secretary an opportunity to pass on her wish to appoint me to the Fourth Activities Committee, a membership group charged with making a critical study of ALA's organization and programs.

I passed scrutiny, was duly appointed, and attended the first postwar conference, held at Buffalo in 1946. Members of the Activities Committee were free to sit in on all committee and board meetings, and so one day I walked into the Executive Board's session. I was met by silence. No one knew who I was, not even Milam, until I introduced myself and was then greeted with forced cordiality. The committee met a couple of times, chaired by Emerson Greenaway, and then faded away.

It wasn't until David Clift took office as Executive Secretary and ALA had a series of outstanding presidents that the beast suffered any change. I held other committee assignments, and as chairman of the University Libraries section, I staged a lively meeting at a midwinter conference, at which a panel roasted an old chestnut, as to whether a chief librarian should be administrator or bookman. Recalling Maurice Tauber's and my earlier controversy, he as administrator, I as bookman, I suggested we change sides. Whereupon Tauber came with the results of a questionnaire, prepared to speak for an hour, although I had stipulated that twenty minutes was the limit, as there were to be four speakers, chaired by William Dix of Princeton. Tauber did not yield, as I had done years before to Bill Jackson.

This was, is, and I am afraid will ever be the curse of library conferences: speakers' inability to be concise and chairmen's inability to hold them to a time limit. A few years later we arranged a conference on oral and written library reporting, during which various speakers stressed the need and means to be brief. The proceedings were brilliantly edited by Betty Rosenberg and published as a UCLA Library Occasional Paper called *Mean What You Say*.

I served two four-year terms on the ALA Council, once as an elected member-at-large, the other time as the California Library Association's councillor, and in those eight years I made one contribution to the professional welfare. It was at a midwinter conference. Council opened with the President reporting the Executive Board's decision to withdraw support from its official *Intellectual Freedom Newsletter*. No voice was raised. I looked at Everett Moore. His face was flushed. He was angry to the point of speechlessness. I rose and demanded an explanation, followed by Moore, Vosper, and Jerome Cushman of Kansas and New Orleans. The result was the giving to Everett Moore of monthly space in the *ALA Bulletin* for a column on intellectual freedom and censorship, a feature which brought him a national reputation as a fair and effective spokesman. I regret never having served on the International Relations Committee, where my experience in foreign countries would have made me useful.

ALA and the profession benefitted increasingly from

several strong editors: Samray Smith of the *ALA Bulletin* and the two British imports, Eric Moon of the *Library Journal* and John Wakeman of the *Wilson Library Bulletin;* and of course the nonpareil Sol Malkin who with his wife Mary Ann made the *Antiquarian Bookman* the liveliest of all library literature. Thanks to Moon and Wakeman, the sorry business of library racial segregation was brought into the open and dealt with by the ALA.

During the editorship of Marie Loizeaux, I contributed frequently to the *Wilson Library Bulletin*, and was asked by her, and later by John Wakeman, to write a regular column. The timing was never right. Harry Bauer wrote the column, followed by Jesse Shera, two masters of the short form.

The timing was right when Eric Moon asked me to write a monthly column in the *Library Journal*. I agreed to contribute "On the Grindstone" for a year only. Among the ones I wrote was one for the late Frederick P. Keppel who, as head of the Carnegie Foundation, did so much for libraries and library education. This he did as a perceptive, authoritative individual. Library philanthropy today is more apt to be hog-tied by committees and overly concerned with technology.

Eric Moon proved to be a good friend and an honest critic. Although he promised complete freedom to write as I wished, he did balk at one of my columns. Called "Go Forth and Be Useful," it was originally a graduation address to one of the library school classes. Moon found it obnoxious. I recalled his promise and held him to it. I had more response to it from readers than to any other of my columns.

My closest editorial colleague was Everett Moore. I wrote regularly for the *UCLA Librarian* which, under his editorship, became one of the best library staff publications. Together we founded the UCLA Library's Occasional Papers series, and we were also associated on the board of the *California Librarian,* the quarterly of the state association, which kept improving under a succession of able editors: Bertha Marshall, Neal Harlow, Ray Holt, William Eshelman, and Henry Madden. As designed by Ward Ritchie, it became the handsomest of all library publications. It repeatedly won national awards for content and format.

When Kathleen Molz became editor of the *Wilson Library Bulletin* we had the following conversation:

M. "It has been a long time since you appeared in the *Wilson.*"

P. "It has been a long time since anyone asked me to."

M. "I had the idea you belonged to *LJ.*"

P. "I always had to force Eric to publish me. Why don't you ask me for something?"

She never did. A pity for us both. Miss Molz transformed the *Wilson* into a beautiful and readable periodical. Everett Moore is on its editorial board, and so I don't feel entirely left out.

I was deluded once to seek the presidency of the ALA. This was following my keynote address in 1952. I was rooming at the Waldorf with Donald Coney and before we went to sleep that night, after my ballroom address to 4,000 members, Coney said, "You can go all the way now."

That was apparently as far as he went on my behalf. Andrew Horn launched a campaign the next year for my nomination. The result was a rebuke from the chairman of the nominating committee who declared that the letters he had received from librarians recruited by Horn obviously represented a synthetic enthusiasm. Years later this chairman phoned us in Malibu and asked if he could bring a friend by for tea. We made them welcome. All was forgiven—and the friend was a beauty.

When the chairman of a later committee asked if they could place my name on the ballot for president, I declined. It was too late. The Library School was due to open. I was needed there, and there I remained for the rest of my career.

It was in 1960 that the ALA conferred on me the first Clarence Day Award for the encouragement of a love of books and reading, actually the service I was best suited for. I was in London, on the way home from a trip around the world, when I received a cable from Milton Lord, Director of the Boston Public Library and chairman of the Award Committee, and so I flew to Montreal where the ALA was meeting in its annual conference under the presidency of my namesake, Benjamin Powell of Duke University Library. As president of the Canadian Library Association, Neal Harlow was also on the platform when I received the $1,000 and an etching of my choice. I believe my breezy manner embarrassed Bostonian Lord, as when I rose to accept the award and said only "Dear Ben, good Lord, great Day!"

My final service to the ALA came when President Edwin Castagna, one of the best librarians of our time and a long-time colleague in California before he became librarian of the Enoch Pratt, asked me to keynote the annual conference at Detroit in 1965 with "Great Land of Libraries." In the words of Eric Moon it, as did all of my major addresses, "left the audience incredibly divided." Yet even those who took the opposite side, listened to what I said, which was enough for me.

By this time I no longer had the patience to work in an organization as large and complex as the ALA had become. I derived vicarious satisfaction from seeing Edwin Castagna and Robert Vosper serve as successive presidents. Both were Sydney Mitchell protégés. It was sad that he did not live to see them become national leaders and spokesmen. Their success would not have astonished him.

As for the Association of American Library Schools, I can say nothing either for or against it. It is a nonentity. After serving as its president, this was also the opinion of Dean Jesse Shera, an unusual instance of his slowness to learn.

I can say little about the Special Libraries Association. Though a member, I found their publications and meetings intellectually arid. Their chief concerns were technical. Following a controversy in their publication *Sci-Tech News*, in which I took on a dozen or more correspondents and doubtless gained no converts, SLA asked me to keynote their 1963 San Francisco conference.

"Into the Mainstream" was a call to special librarians to engage in the intellectual and cultural life of their communities. I spoke in the Rose Room of the Palace Hotel and was moved by memories of dancing in that room, years before, to the music of Art Hickman's orchestra and his "Rose Room" theme. I brought the audience to its feet with my peroration, calling on them first to be librarians, then specialists, to swim in the mainstream of culture, rather than in the backwaters of technology.

I was active in the Association of Research Libraries, serving four years on its executive board and in the final year as its chairman. The proceedings never engaged me deeply, except for some brushes I had with Keyes Metcalf who was continually proposing special commissions, inquiries, and conferences. The best thing I did in ARL was to chair a subcommittee on customs procedure which led to simplification of the incredibly archaic American entry procedures. Most of the credit for this was due to Vosper, who dug up the facts and figures.

What I enjoyed most in the ARL was friendship with kindred spirits such as James Babb of Yale, Luther Evans and Verner Clapp of the Library of Congress, David Jonah of Brown University, Stanley Pargellis of the Newberry Library, Robert Miller of Indiana University, and Charles David of the University of Pennsylvania. The climax came in 1953 when we played host to the ARL at the Clark Library and offered bar service, with Andrew Horn as tender, and a steak dinner. It was an evening of elegance and abundance.

Professional organizations have a common life cycle. They begin as small clusters of gregarious, dedicated individuals, gradually grow, proliferate, subdivide, and depersonalize, and become powerful, useful, necessary—and tedious in their involved proceedings. Thus did the American Library Association and its offshoot, the Special Libraries Association. As it began to happen to the Association of Research Libraries, I lost interest, reconciled to seeing younger, eager organization men take over.

I did not want to let happen to me what happened to Nathan van Patten, librarian of Stanford University for twenty years, a bibliographical "loner" lost in any large organization. At the New York conference in 1952, I saw him seated in a corner of the Waldorf lobby, beside a potted palm. He beckoned to me. "I'm lonesome," he said, "sit and talk with me." What he really meant was for me to sit and listen to him talk. I did, spellbound by the way his cigarette stuck to his moving lower lip as his monologue droned on, his massive Dutch face wreathed in smoke. What made his talk hearable was that it was always about books, ranging from Arthur Machen to Greenland imprints and Mexican obstetrical literature.

The national organization which meant the most to me, and in which I became the only Western president, was the BSA, the Bibliographical Society of America.

Upon perceiving early that the society was dominated by New York and New England, I spoke out at a meeting in Philadelphia that there was a need for regionalization. I proposed to organize a rump section on the Pacific Coast. The proposal led to my being elected to the society's governing council and becoming president during the biennium 1954–56.

During my tenure in office, in addition to the annual meeting in New York, spring meetings were held in Chicago, Ann Arbor, Charlottesville, and Washington, and most memorable, a summer meeting in California at the Huntington Library. We elected the first women members of the Council: Frances Hamill, who was also an antiquarian bookseller, and Dorothy Schullian, Librarian of the National Library of Medicine's historical collection.

At the Chicago meeting we brought from retirement J. Christian Bay, the great Danish bookman who had headed the John Crerar Library, and whose *Fortunes of Books* was high on my list of favorite reading. Then about eighty-five years old, Dr. Bay presented a model paper to the meeting in the Newberry Library, skillfully composed and beautifully read and of exactly the right length. This meeting also featured Frances Hamill's paper on early Chicago women booksellers.

The Council met at a dinner meeting that evening in my room at the Palmer House, and it was one of the gayest gatherings that body ever held, at least in my time. Present were Mary and Donald Hyde, Cornelia and Waller Barrett, and Fritz Liebert. I went on to catch a 1:30 A.M. flight west and was asleep before takeoff.

Conservative members on the Council warned that a summer meeting in California would be poorly attended. As far as they were concerned, they were right. Liebert was the only one to make the trip. The meeting was one of the largest in the society's history, drawing more than usually attended the annual conference in New York. An outstanding paper was read by Jake Zeitlin, called "Small Renaissance, Southern California-Style," in which he gave a résumé of what had been happening in the book arts.

Guest of honor at the luncheon, held in Caltech's Athenaeum, was the venerable Henry R. Wagner, then in his early nineties. He was wheeled in a chair by Edwin H. Carpenter and although nearly blind, his hearing enabled him to bask in Liebert's luncheon speech, a tribute to Wagner as the oldest living member of the society and graduate of Yale in the class of 1884. That was one of the finest days of my life, a peak I was not to surmount until four years later when the Library School was dedicated.

The BSA gave me many bookish friendships, with Tom Streeter, Jackson, Babb, the Lieberts, the Hydes, the Barretts, the John Gordans, Curt Buhlers, Fred Adamses, Leroy Kimball, Robert G. Vail, Alexander Davidson, and latterly with the Misses Hamill and Schullian, Robert Metzdorf, Robert Taylor, Frederick Goff, Edwin Wolf and others. A high point was the Council dinner held at the Grolier Club after the annual meeting. Presidents of the society became ex officio Council members for life, a gracious recognition of lasting fraternity.

Although I enjoyed these associations with the country's bibliographical leaders and membership in the Grolier Club, I remained a Westerner in mind and manner, thankful that fortune had kept me in California, a region where my compulsive style was more needed and better tolerated than it would have been in Cambridge or Manhattan.

These Eastern trips also were buying trips, as I made the rounds of antiquarian bookshops in New York, Boston, Philadelphia and Washington. On my visit to the capital in 1946—it was the first time I had been back since we left for California in 1910—I went to the Department of Agriculture building to see the bronze wall plaque which commemorated my father's pioneer work in the department.

In New York the kindness of Jim Babb, Fritz Liebert, or Fred Adams gave me lodging at the Yale Club, and I also came through books to friendship with Ben Grauer, NBC's senior announcer whose Toscanini broadcasts I had long followed.

The California Library Association also saw me active as a member, committee man, and officer. I served as president in 1950, having risen through local and regional assignments, the most important of which had been to head a committee which reformed the society's quarterly bulletin and transformed it into the *California Librarian*.

I ran twice for president before I was elected. After the war, Tom Dabagh and I were defeated by Eleanor Wilson, Librarian of Kern County. This was again my good fortune, for the year when I was elected to the presidency was California's centennial year of statehood, and I was able to link our annual conference with the state-sponsored literary centennial celebration at a joint meeting held in Sacramento. Gustave Arlt had been named by the Governor as director of the centennial celebration, and we collaborated in planning a program that is still held up as a model of what a library conference can be.

California's library association recognizes the size of the state by dividing itself into regional districts, and I spent many weekends that spring in travelling to these regional meetings, building toward the climax in June of the state conference in Sacramento. State Librarian Mabel R. Gillis, daughter of the California library pioneer, James L. Gillis, also attended these district meetings, and I thus gained an opportunity of winning my way into her confidence to the degree that I became her choice to succeed her as State Librarian.

We had started out badly in 1939 when, encouraged by my experience with the Cowan collection, I had taken the state civil service examination for the position of senior Californiana librarian in the State Library. The written part was followed by an oral examination, the chief examiner being Miss Gillis.

I confess to inner trembling when I faced her across the table in the State Building in downtown Los Angeles. Short, formidable, her face seamed, her narrow eyes hooded, she appeared a grim guardian of the books. Her first question was not aimed to put me at ease.

"Why are you taking this examination?"

"To win a place on the list."

"Now tell me the truth, Dr. Powell, aren't you using this to advance your position at UCLA?"

"That hadn't occurred to me," I answered truthfully, having come to the knowledge that nothing would advance me on Goodwin's organization chart.

Miss Gillis did not relent. "If you are offered the position, will you move to Sacramento?"

"Try me and see," was my flip reply.

Her eyes narrowed and I thought she was going to push the table over on me. Then they widened. "You're a bit of a rogue," she said, with the faintest of smiles.

I passed the examination and placed fourth on a list of five. First place, and the position, went to Neal Harlow.

Now eleven years later Miss Gillis and I were stumping the state together. At the district meetings she talked libraries and I talked California literature and history. We were in Eureka, Quincy, Columbia, Berkeley, Marysville, and Pomona, liking one another more all the time. I made friends among librarians, trustees, and plain citizens interested in libraries, as I spoke not as a Southerner or an Angeleno, but as a statewide Californian.

I also visited my parents-in-law, Otie and R. K. Shoemaker, who had moved from Kansas City to Los Molinos in the northern Sacramento Valley. Otie is still there to this day, nearing ninety, a most wonderful old lady.

On the way home one Sunday morning, waiting for a change of planes at the San Francisco airport, I read in the *Chronicle* of the death of Provost Clarence Dykstra, the great-hearted, big Frisian Dutchman who had given me everything I needed and asked for. He and his radiant wife Lillian had flooded the UCLA campus with the warmth and affection so often lacking in administrators. I sat there with tears in my eyes, hating to believe that Dyke was gone. Ten years were to pass before Franklin Murphy created a comparable ambience at UCLA.

My local arrangements chairman for the Sacramento Conference was Frederick Wemmer, Sacramento County Librarian, a sophisticated librarian and a good organizer. We planned the program with attention to quality and detail. From the East we brought Clarence "Skip" Graham, Librarian of the Louisville, Kentucky Public Library, who had defeated Carl Milam as the Keyes Metcalf group's choice for the presidency of the ALA. Chief Assistant Librarian of Congress Verner Clapp also came as a speaker. We had Phil Townsend Hanna, Editor of *Westways*, to speak at a luncheon in honor of the State Library's centennial. Miss Gillis had the place of honor, of course, and tears were in her eyes as Hanna paid tribute to her father. Idwal Jones spoke on California folklore, John Walton Caughey on history, Joseph P. Knowland on journalism, Richard Lillard on literature. It was a great week, culminating in a banquet in the Senator Hotel at which Dixon Wecter, as the speaker on the literary centennial, was to be introduced by President Robert Gordon Sproul. This was preceded by a cocktail party given by Ruth and Elmer Belt, Mrs. Belt then serving as a trustee of the Los Angeles Public Library.

And so the week moved to the climax of the Sproul-Wecter program. The latter's address was one of the most eloquent ever heard in California, and after it was over Fay and I joined the Wecters, Dixon and Elizabeth, in the bar for a nightcap. Soon they excused themselves for a walk in the tree-filled capitol park across the street before turning in, and Fay and I went to bed.

I was awakened by the phone sometime after midnight. It was Elizabeth Wecter.

"Larry, please come. Dixon has had a heart attack."

I slipped on robe and slippers and hurried to their room two floors below. Firemen were leaving the room with oxygen equipment. I entered and saw a dead man on the bed. It was Dixon Wecter, his strong face peaceful, noble—and cold. The house doctor was packing his bag, preparing to leave. Elizabeth, in her nightgown, seized my hand. "Larry, do something. Please do something. He can't be dead."

I picked up the phone and asked for Dr. Belt. I also called Fay to come right down. Dr. Belt arrived at once, in robe and slippers. He examined the body on the bed, then put his arm around Elizabeth. "He's gone," he said. "Try to be brave."

Fay arrived and comforted Elizabeth. I phoned to Arlt's room and asked him to break the news to President Sproul and also to have a Berkeley undertaker come for the body. I removed the wristwatch and wedding ring from Wecter's body and drew the sheet over his face. On the bureau was Elizabeth's corsage and a love note from her husband. They were a beautiful couple.

I remembered a call I had received from Wecter two weeks before the conference, asking to be relieved of the speaking assignment, saying that as editor of the Mark Twain estate he was pressed almost beyond endurance. "The program is being printed," I told him, "and it is not possible to replace you at this late date." He reluctantly agreed, performed brilliantly, and now lay dead under the sheet. I am still haunted by the memory.

In the morning Fay took orange juice and coffee to Elizabeth Wecter's room and we prepared to drive her to Berkeley in the Wecter car, Vosper driving ours after us and I then taking Bob to the San Francisco airport for his flight home. Fay and I went on to the Hot Springs on the Big Sur coast for a couple of days of rest.

That ended my year with CLA. A Guggenheim Fellowship and a sabbatical leave to study the antiquarian book trade were to take Fay and me to England for 1950–51, with Vosper to act as University Librarian.

Before leaving for Europe late in August I made a flying one-day trip to Sacramento to confer with Miss Gillis.

"You are the one to succeed me," she said, as we were closeted in her panelled office. "You have won the hearts of librarians throughout the state."

"I love them dearly." I said, "and this whole great beautiful state. But I am committed to return to UCLA for at least a year after my sabbatical leave. I will consider it, if you will stay in office another two years."

She agreed, and I flew back to Los Angeles.

While in New York before sailing in the *Queen Elizabeth,* we spent a weekend with Fred and Betty Adams at their home in the Berkshires, just over the hills from my father's natal Ghent, and Fred took me to see "Arrowhead," the farm where Melville wrote *Moby Dick.* I received an acceptance letter from the *Pacific Spectator,* the quarterly to which I had sent "Music into

Silence," an essay about my earlier musical life. Written by Edith Mirrielees, the editor, it was one of the most encouraging letters of my life.

I have written about that year in *The Alchemy of Books*. It forged a bond between us and Great Britain and gave us British friends for life. The UCLA and Clark libraries were enriched by many thousands of books and manuscripts. I also collected a great librarian in persuading Robert L. Collison to come to UCLA for a year as a Reference Librarian. Then head of the Central Reference Library in Westminster and due eventually to become Librarian of the BBC, Rob Collison, author, lecturer, wit, is the best reference librarian I have ever known.

The year's leave also enabled me to complete the manuscript of my first book of essays, *Islands of Books*. Published in 1951 by Ward Ritchie, it was composed of my contributions to *Hoja Volante*, the quarterly of the Zamorano Club which had been revived under the editorship of W. W. Robinson, whose persuasiveness had resulted in a series of essays I wrote for this periodical. I gratefully dedicated the book to him.

Another friend of my writing was Caroline Anderson, the widow of Ritchie's partner, Gregg Anderson, whose death in the Normandy invasion cost fine printing one of its ablest practitioners and us a dear friend. Caroline inherited her husband's share in the press, and to an editorial role she brought knowledge and taste. In 1966, I acquired some of her interest and thus became a junior partner in the Ward Ritchie Press. He and I had begun our careers together and we were due to end them likewise, another instance of friendship and fortune in perfect conjunction.

In the spring of 1951, before we had returned home, I received the news that Miss Gillis had announced her retirement at the end of the calendar year 1951. This was six months before the agreed time. I also began to receive urgent letters from Fritz Wemmer who was heading an informal group to back me to succeed Miss Gillis. I replied that I was committed to remain at UCLA at least until July 1, 1952.

Then I heard from Harold L. Hamill, City Librarian of Los Angeles, that he had been appointed by the Governor as chairman of the committee to recommend a successor to Miss Gillis. Donald Coney was another member of the committee. Hamill wanted me to cable if I would agree to letting my name be included among those to be considered. I cabled back one word YES.

When we reached New York on the way home, I found a telegram from Hamill, asking me to phone him. I did so. Interviews of candidates were to be held soon in San Francisco, would I attend? I explained my commitment to the university, but that I would present myself for interview. Fay flew on home and I began a cross-country journey in a Hillman, my mind turning with the wheels, seeking the way which was not clear to me.

What should I do? I knew I could have a long useful career as State Librarian, serving as a spokesman, as I had done in 1950, for literature, history, and librarianship, in all of which California was incomparably rich. I also remembered my pledge to Regent Dickson that I would turn to the matter of the Library School at UCLA at the time when I thought the campus was ready. That time was near. I had persuaded the Library Council to recommend to the President that an expert be brought in to make a study of the need for an additional school at UCLA.

After my return to Los Angeles, Fay and I set out by car for the interview the next day in San Francisco. That evening in Berkeley I left her at the hotel and went to see Mitchell. He was old and ill and not far from death, but he took my dilemma and revolved it slowly as we sought to resolve it.

"If you go to Sacramento," he concluded, "you can forget the library school. There will never be one there."

"Will there be one at UCLA?"

"If you are convinced that there is a need."

"Is there a need?"

"You are the one to answer that."

I said good night and drove to the Western Union office in downtown Berkeley and sent a night letter to Harold Hamill at the State Building in San Francisco, withdrawing as candidate. Then I got the first good night's sleep in a long while, and in the morning we turned around and drove back the four hundred miles to Los Angeles. That was the last time I saw Mitchell.

Everett Moore, Betty Rosenberg, and I edited and persuaded the CLA to publish Mitchell's memoirs. He had begun to write them after his retirement, urged by Donald Coney, August Frugé, and me, and had brought them up to the period of his coming to Berkeley in 1912. Then he died, leaving them unfinished. All we had was a recording, made by Andrew Horn and Neal Harlow, of Mitchell's reminiscences of the role he had played in library education; and this we transcribed and used as a final chapter—better than nothing.

Throughout the years since finishing at Dijon in 1932, I kept in touch with Professor Georges Connes. In 1948 he came to California and I had the pleasure of driving him the length of the state, visiting Dean Mitchell in Berkeley, the Jeffers in Carmel, and Henry Miller in Big Sur. In 1957 Fay and I went to Dijon for a reunion with the Connes, and on a cold October afternoon when we were kept indoors by rain, Connes took me to his attic study and showed me the enormous manuscript of his translation of "The Ring and the Book," the first time Browning's masterpiece had been rendered in French. The labor had occupied him throughout the Occupation when, as a member of the Resistance, he had had a couple of dangerous escapes from the Gestapo. Now it seemed hopeless to obtain a French publisher, the one in Belgium that had engaged to do it having gone bankrupt.

Back in California I approached my friends in the San Francisco Browning Society, a group to which I had been lecturing every year, and together with similar groups elsewhere in America, they pledged enough money to persuade Gallimard to publish Connes' translation. I felt that I had thereby somewhat repaid the debt owed Georges Connes for his kindness of a quarter-century before.

MY LIFE AS A "COMMUNIST"

My left-wing period, more pink than red, lasted for two years, 1934–36, and was caused by the Depression and our family losses, and also by my uncertainty and insecurity while working in the book trade. The riches of experience that I was amassing bore interest only in later years. I was disillusioned by the collapse of our economic system. In 1928, the first time I had been old enough to vote, I naturally chose Herbert Hoover, my father's friend, whose inscribed picture "To Lawrence Powell from Herbert Hoover" was one of my prized possessions. In France I was voteless and could claim no part in the Roosevelt landslide. Upon registering in 1934, I declared my affiliation to be Communist. It was an idealistic gesture. I knew no Communists, never attended any meetings, or took part in politics of any kind. Fay said it was a foolish thing to do, and she registered as a Democrat.

Time proved her right. Foolishness became scandalous seventeen years later when the Los Angeles newspapers carried front-page headlines "UCLA LIBRARIAN A COMMUNIST." If ever I were to be destroyed, it could have been then. When the story first broke, my closest associate, Vosper, concluded that I henceforth had limited usefulness as spokesman for intellectual freedom. He was wrong. The disclosure had the opposite effect. Conservatives came to my defense. Liberals were silent. Fortune and friendship rose to the zenith. It was an ordeal that gave me new strength and peace. Henceforth I had no fear of the future.

A Committee on Education of the State Senate was conducting an inquiry into teacher training by California's several colleges and universities, and had directed fire at UCLA for its alleged left-wing leanings. This was an old chestnut, often reroasted by the local newspapers, and was due to a small noisy minority of students and a few faculty. Actually the UCLA community was conservative, as much later events at Berkeley were to demonstrate.

While this Senate inquiry was occurring, a liberal young junior member of Everett Moore's reference staff put up a bulletin board display of current periodical articles critical of legislative inquiries. Some students or faculty, or both, apparently wrote to the Senate Committee, drawing attention to the display. The committee put an investigator to work, seeking subversive elements in the UCLA Library. They found me. Digging back through voter registration records, they found that in 1934, while resident at 2303 Loma Vista Place, Los Angeles, I had registered to vote as a Communist.

I knew none of this or even remembered the incident, when I was subpoenaed to appear before the Senate Committee at the State Building in downtown Los Angeles. Nor did I know that the headline-hungry committee had released its news to the local press, in advance of my appearance, so that the afternoon and evening papers could have the story. They had also tipped off Andrew Hamilton, head of the UCLA news bureau, who phoned me that morning—the hearing was at 11:00 —and urged me to get into my testimony, as quickly as possible, facts about my parentage and local upbringing. He gave no hint of what was to come.

Everett Moore and John Smith, head of the Acquisitions Department, accompanied me to the State Building, and were in the packed audience when I took the stand. Chairman of the committee was Senator Nelson Dilworth, an elderly, walrus-moustached figure, who represented the citrus area of Hemet and Riverside. I began to see what Hamilton had meant, and when the committee's counsel, who was conducting the questioning, asked me who I was, I identified myself as the son of G. Harold Powell, the late General Manager of the California Fruit Growers Exchange. At that point Senator Dilworth interrupted his counsel, leaned toward me and asked,

"Do you mean to say that you are Harold Powell's son?"

"Yes, Senator, I was the youngest of three boys."

Dilworth beckoned the counsel to him and they whispered back and forth. The hearing went on.

"You were in Europe this past year, were you not?" the counsel asked.

"I was a Guggenheim Fellow."

"What contacts did you make?"

"Bookshops and restaurants and an occasional cathedral."

The audience laughed and Senator Dilworth rapped for order.

Then the counsel tossed his bombshell. Handing me a photostat, he asked, "Is that your signature?"

I saw the trap. It was a photostat of the voters registration book of 1934, and there was my signature and my declared affiliation as Communist. I rolled with the punch.

"Yes," I admitted. "That is my signature."

"That's all," the counsel said.

I addressed myself to Dilworth.

"Senator, may I have a chance to explain?"

The counsel interrupted. "I hardly think an explanation is necessary."

Dilworth motioned to me to speak, and in as few words as possible, I described the disillusioned idealism that had led me from right to left, that I had not been a Communist, had known none, nor had attended any kind of party gathering, and from 1936 on had been a registered Democrat. The Senator allowed me to speak without interruption from his counsel, then adjourned the hearing, and beckoned me to his chair.

"I knew your father," he said. "He helped me get started in citrus. He was a very fine man."

"I am sorry I had to meet my father's friend under these circumstances," I said.

"Don't worry, boy," the old gentleman said. "Call on me if I can ever be of help to you."

As I left the hearing chamber, I passed a group of older men and women. "You red rat," one of the women screamed and spat on me.

Moore, Smith, and Hamilton were waiting outside. We crossed the street to a restaurant.

"Good going," Hamilton said. "I'll never forget Dilworth's face when he heard you were Harold Powell's son."

"What do you suppose he whispered to his counsel?"

"I'd like to think it was a wish to call the whole thing off."

It was too late of course. As we left the restaurant, the *Evening Herald* was being sold, with its banner headline UCLA LIBRARIAN A COMMUNIST.

Upon Hamilton's advice, I returned to campus, wrote out the explanation given the committee, dittoed copies, and circulated it to my own staff. Hamilton in turn rushed it out as a press release, with copies to members of the Board of Regents, with the result that the night and morning papers carried this statement. It was an example of the swift and skillful work Andy Hamilton always turned out. In all our years together, he never failed to serve me and the library well.

The next thing I did was to telephone Fay what had happened and that I was O.K. Then I telephoned Acting Provost Vern Knudsen, the acoustical physicist, and told him. "Phone Sproul," he said, "and tell him I'm back of you 100 per cent."

I got through to the President in Berkeley, and I shall never forget the groan which preceded his "Oh no!" But he listened to my explanation, assured me of his backing, then urged me to inform Regent Dickson.

I didn't have time to do so. As I hung up from talking with the President, Miss Bradstreet ushered Regent Dickson into my office. He came to my desk as I rose, put his arm around me, and said with great tenderness, "Don't worry, son, I'm back of you."

He was indeed. At the next meeting of the Regents, when Governor Knight raised the question about "that Communist librarian at UCLA," according to President Sproul who told me the story afterward, Chairman Dickson replied, "Mr. Governor, I wish to vouch personally for Dr. Powell. His heritage and character are known to me. Shall we proceed to the next order of business?"

I had one more ordeal before that long day was over. I was due to speak at a dinner meeting of Pasadena's Twilight Club, composed of the community's elder statesmen in the arts and sciences and public affairs. Before driving to the Annandale Country Club, I was persuaded by Andy Horn to go with him to the staff room for a snack; and while I sought to gather my forces, Andy made a pot of tea and rustled up a sandwich and a banana. He also offered to chauffeur me if I didn't feel up to the drive. I was touched by his kindness, as I had been by Elizabeth Bradstreet's upon my return to campus.

I reached the club as they were about to sit down for dinner. The first person to greet me was my old Occidental nemesis, Dean Cleland, now retired and a member of the Huntington Library staff and, I must say, wonderfully mellowed. He grinned and shook my hand and said, "The lengths some men will go to get in the headlines!"

I felt better. I was introduced after dinner by the club's president, Robert O. Schad, curator of rare books in the Huntington Library, who said,

"Gentlemen, whatever you may read about Larry Powell—and he's always breaking into print—I want you to know that he is my old friend." To warm applause I embraced Schad and launched into an account of my book buying in Britain. It was one of the best talks I ever gave.

As I left the Annandale to drive home, I turned on the car's radio and heard the Toscanini recording of the Mozart *Divertimento*, K. 387, and that divine music comforted me like a warm shower.

I stopped at my mother's cottage in Westwood for a cup of tea. She had heard the news, and my statement, on the radio. Fay was waiting up for me and I had another cup of tea, as I recounted the day's events. She reported that Dorothy Drake of Scripps and Clara Breed, City Librarian of San Diego, had driven in from Claremont that evening to offer their love and support. Sufficient unto the day . . . I fell asleep.

The next morning I had a visit from Edgar J. Goodspeed, the Bible translator, and a rock-ribbed Republican.

"Larry," he said, "I am shocked to learn that you are a—Democrat. I always thought you were one of us."

Another staunch conservative who came forward in friendship and support was Dwight L. Clarke, the banker-bookman-historian and colleague in the Zamorano Club, whose wife Edna also never failed to show affection for Fay and me.

Later I did call on Senator Dilworth for help, at the time the UCLA Library's stack addition was up for legislative funding. Time and again it had been side-tracked by Berkeley's higher priorities, but now it had reached the Senate Finance Committee, on which Nelson Dilworth sat. The university lobbyist alerted me that Dilworth was going to vote against it. I reached him by phone.

"This is Harold Powell's son," I said. "I need your help."

"What is it, boy?"

"UCLA urgently needs that stack addition."

There was a long silence before he spoke.

"I'll give it my personal attention," was the reply.

I heard later from the university's lobbyist that it was Dilworth's abstention from voting, either way, that had assured passage of our funding bill. Thus he succeeded in serving both conscience and Harold Powell's son.

The painful lesson I learned from this experience was that one has to face, sooner or later, the consequences of his acts.

AT THE MOTHER OF LIBRARY SCHOOLS

I have sought to write about the decisive and important forces and events in my life and not to pad this memoir with names and trivia. My life has been overflowing with people and places, many things happening concurrently on several fronts, so that I have had to choose what seemed to me, as I recall them, the matters worth writing about. I realize that a biographer, if I ever have one, may well regard as more meaningful events I have slighted or forgotten.

The semester I spent at Columbia University in the spring of 1954, teaching in the School of Library Service, was one of those watershed times, after which everything flowed toward the UCLA school to be founded five years later. A leave of absence granted by Chancellor Raymond Allen was for the purpose of studying library school organization and operation. It also gave me my first opportunity of classroom teaching since the semester, twenty-four years earlier, when I conducted a class at Occidental in "dumb-bell English," as the remedial course was called.

How did it happen that I went to Columbia? It was one man's idea, and one he had held since 1949 when he offered me a professorship on the Columbia faculty. He was Dean Carl M. White of the library school. We had been fellow speakers on the program at the San Francisco ALA conference in 1939, when I gave my paper on "The Functions of Rare Books." White was then University Librarian at Urbana, Illinois, having come from a similar post at New York University, then moved on to become both University Librarian and Dean at Columbia and finally Dean alone. Although a poor administrator, given to theoretical verbalizing, perhaps from having taken a Ph.D. in philosophy at Cornell, he was a gentleman, scholar, and a kind person. At the ALA conference at Atlantic City in 1949, we walked the boardwalk while he sounded me on coming to Columbia. "Not permanently," I said, "but when you have a semester's vacancy, let me know."

That Atlantic City conference is memorable also for being the last time I saw Dr. Rosenbach and his brother Philip. I had come by way of Philadelphia and stayed overnight with the brothers at their home in De Lancey Place. There I saw books and manuscripts to dazzle mine eyes. We drove next day to Atlantic City, and en route the Doctor offered the Clark the original manuscript of Oscar Wilde's *Salome* for $7,500. And I turned it down. *Mea culpa.*

Robert Miller of Indiana had arranged a program on rare books, at which he and I and John Cook Wyllie of Virginia read papers. Dr. Rosenbach was in the audience, probably the first, last, and only ALA conference he ever attended.

He and Philip were staying at their place down shore, and asked me to bring a few congenials to lunch the next day, to ride down in the car they would send for us. I rounded up Bob Miller, Charlie David, and Carl White. The Doctor was on the wagon and a bit subdued, and let Philip run the show. The lunch was perfect.

And thus I went to Columbia as Visiting Professor to take the place of Lowell Martin who had gone to Rutgers to head the new library school. I was expected to teach Martin's course in "Theory and Practice of Library Administration" and to conduct his doctoral seminar in "Special Problems in Library Planning and Operation." Dean White arranged the program so that I taught on Monday and Wednesday mornings and held the seminar on Wednesday evening, leaving me free the rest of the week.

I travelled and spoke throughout the spring, with lectures at and visits to the University of Tennessee, Duke University, University of North Carolina, Georgia Tech, Emory University, Agnes Scott College, University of Georgia, Princeton University, Johns Hopkins University, University of Maryland, Brown University, Trinity College, Simmons College, Yale University, and Indiana University.

White's faculty was an odd group. Tauber and I were polite to one another. Allen Hazen, the bibliographer, was immersed in his own research. Sweet Miriam Tompkins died soon after I arrived. The "wolf in the flock" was Robert D. Leigh, the sociologist-surveyor, former President of Bennington College, whom the Library Council had retained in California two years before to survey the need for a library school at UCLA and whose recommendation had been negative. While in California he had privately voiced the opinion that it was all impure politics, merely the personal ambition of Larry Powell. Later, after Leigh had replaced White as Dean and was encouraging White to leave Columbia, I learned that Leigh had been the only member of the Columbia faculty who had opposed my appointment, even as visiting professor for a semester. To me, however, he was all smiles. His office door bore the cryptic legend "The Communications Study." Two members of the university library staff were especially cordial and helpful: Roland Baughman, head of Special Collections, formerly at the Huntington Library, and Darthula Wilcox, head of the library school library, a no-nonsense Texan from Austin.

It had been painful leaving home. Norman was working for a year, before attending UCLA, and Wilkie was still in high school. Fay decided she could not leave them to be with me in New York. In fact, she felt that I should not leave, that it was a kind of abandonment. I believed that I must go, that it was an opportunity I might never have again. I kept hearing Mitchell's words—he had died the year before—"There will be a library school if you can establish the need." The Leigh report was a roadblock and the Columbia appointment offered a way around it.

Fortune beckoned me to follow. And so I went, first to the ALA midwinter meeting in Chicago, at which I read a paper on Sydney Mitchell, one of the best things I ever wrote, in which I put everything I was and knew, to establish the homely Dean in the Pantheon where he belonged.

I left Chicago one bitter cold, snowy night on a late plane for New York and flew into Manhattan at sunrise, going later in the day to Carnegie Hall with Aunt Mabel to hear Copland and Mozart, balm to my sore spirit. I had repaid the $75 to my dear old aunt and she loved me again. Throughout the four months in Manhattan, living alone in Marie Loizeaux's apartment on Riverside Drive at 79th, I dined once a week with Mabel Satterlee and we went to concerts together and were close in companionship. She loved music and art, and had a gay spirit.

I also saw Ben Grauer at intervals and through his kindness attended Toscanini's farewell broadcast, during which the aged maestro nearly cracked up. It was the time of the McCarthy hearings, a sorry period in our national life. I remember going into the Columbia bookstore once and in a biography of McCarthy finding my name in the index as a Communist sympathizer. It was also during the Columbia bicentennial, and I was continually refreshed and proud to be on campus then in that time of "The Freedom to Know." Carl White and his wife Ruth were unfailingly kind, and when during the Easter recess Fay came back for a week, the Whites gave a reception in our honor and invited us for dinner at their home in New Jersey. In a rented car Fay and I drove up the west bank of the Hudson to my mother's birthplace in Cornwall, in the lee of Storm King, on to Poughkeepsie and visits to the Vassar Library and Roosevelt's grave at Hyde Park. My father's grave was farther up river at Ghent, in the apple country, but darkness was falling and we were due back in New York for dinner.

The supreme experience of the spring was to develop my gifts as a teacher, both in the class of thirty-five and the seminar of eight. The years of lecturing had prepared me. I held the students from the first, as I poured out knowledge and belief in a flood of feeling.

I also read page proof on *The Alchemy of Books*, in press with Ward Ritchie, and prepared the manuscript of a bibliography of Southwestern fiction to be published the following year by Dawson's Book Shop as *Heart of the Southwest*.

Most of my evenings in Manhattan were spent alone, preparing lectures, playing Haydn-Mozart records brought with me, or listening to my favorite radio station WPAT in Paterson, New Jersey. I was lonely and also happy.

It was on a visit to the Yale University Library, as house guest of the Babbs, that lightning struck. During a morning spent in the History of Medicine collection, comparing their Robert Boyle holdings with ours at the

Clark, that a phone call came from UCLA. It was Acting University Librarian Andrew Horn—Vosper was two years gone to Kansas—telling me that an offer had come from Chapel Hill to be the University Librarian in succession to Charles Rush.

"What shall I do?" Andy asked.

"Go," I said. "But remember, the day will come when I'll need you in the library school."

"O.K. boss. I just wanted to hear your voice."

It was a major loss for me, with both Vosper and Horn gone. Gordon Williams was too new to replace Horn, and besides, his talent was not for personnel work. I needed another person with Andy's feeling for other people and his brilliant mind. Who?

The answer came to me in the night not long after. Page Ackerman, the UCLA social welfare librarian. I tried the idea on Horn when he came through on his way for a quick inspection of Chapel Hill. "Of course!" he said. "Why didn't I think of her?"

Although she was without administrative experience, as Vosper had been, I recognized her potential for management and personnel work from her service the year before as president of the staff association. She was pretty and poised, cool without being cold, and universally respected and liked.

The day after my return to UCLA, I persuaded Miss Ackerman to leave the ranks and become the other Assistant University Librarian. This freed me to go on doing the things that only I could do, which were increasingly, as the 1950's ran out, to teach and to write.

In 1955, upon invitation of Chairman Majl Ewing, I became a lecturer in the Department of English, and for the next five years taught a course called "Libraries and Learning," an introduction to printing, publishing, bookselling, and collecting. It was ideal preparation for the eventual library school course called "Introduction to Librarianship," and it also was a source of recruitment for library work.

One of the best recruits was Kenneth Nesheim who worked first at the Clark, graduated in the first library school class, became a Lilly Library Fellow, then was on the Huntington staff, and went finally to Yale where he is now Assistant Librarian of the Beinecke Library. Throughout my directorship of the Clark, nearly twenty-three years in all, I recruited and trained a succession of young men, such as Nesheim, who today occupy key positions in the Congressional, Huntington, and UCLA libraries.

Nineteen fifty-five was the year of our move to the Malibu coast, to a seaside home and garden twenty-eight miles from campus. It was a lifesaving, life-giving move for Fay and me, and in *The Malibu* I wrote about the poetry and the prose of its meaning for us, the drama of the great fire, the halcyon round of hours. The move broke my long habit of going every day to the library. Henceforth until retirement, Fridays and Sundays were my days to stay home and garden, glean the beach and hills, and write. I went in Saturday mornings to work alone in my closed office, sorting out accumulated printed matter and planning the week's work to come, free of calls and appointments.

I have been asked how I managed to read and write so much, in addition to administration, teaching, travel, and speaking. My answer was always the same: eliminate nonessentials and gain free hours. Each must decide what what for him are the nonessentials. And the second part of my answer: marry a woman of character who will adapt, protect, and nourish with unstinting loyalty and love.

HEART OF THE SOUTHWEST

My keynote address at the
Waldorf opened a door which led into the heart of the
Southwest—Arizona and New Mexico. During the
decade from 1953, I was continually travelling in the
two states, visiting libraries, meeting librarians, giving
talks, writing articles, essays, bibliographies, books. I
succeeded gradually in overcoming the hostility felt by
Arizonians toward a water-thief from Southern California.

The door was opened by one of my Waldorf auditors,
the newly appointed librarian of the University of Arizona, Fleming Bennett, who finding himself responsible a
year later for the program at a Tucson conference of the
Arizona Library Association, invited me to be one of the
speakers. Using J. Frank Dobie's *Guide to Life and
Literature of the Southwest* as a starting point, I wrote a
talk called "This Dry and Wrinkled Land," in which I
discoursed on three key books about the Southwest:
Willa Cather's *Death Comes for the Archbishop*, Will
Levington Comfort's *Apache*, and Haniel Long's *Inter-
linear to Cabeza de Vaca*.

In preparing, delivering and in the response to this talk in mid-April, I experienced another illumination, and suffered a conversion. Afterward, I likened Dobie's book to a burning glass, under which the Southwest caught fire and shone with ineffable refulgence.

Asked to give an address that fall to the Zamorano Club at a banquet honoring Frederick Webb Hodge upon his eighty-ninth birthday, I took to the field in September, trailing through Arizona and New Mexico over the routes followed a generation before by Hodge in his epochal work on Southwestern ethnology and archaeology. Yuma, the Salt River Valley, Fort Wingate, Zuni, Acoma, and the Enchanted Mesa in turn were visited, explored, and climbed, in an itinerary which blended landscape, literature, and history. The result was "Sky, Sun, and Water," a tribute to Hodge and the land; and when I gave the address and the gentle old scholar rose afterward and thanked me, it was one of the peaks of my life.

The appearance of those two talks in the *Southwest Review* and *Arizona Highways* opened new outlets and audiences, and over the next decade I contributed frequently to their columns. They brought new friends, Dobie in Austin (I visited him on my way home from New York in 1954), the printer Carl Hertzog of El Paso, Haniel Long in Santa Fe, Erna Fergusson in Albuquerque and her brother Harvey in Berkeley, and Comfort's daughter Jane in Los Angeles.

And with two library colleagues met in Tucson, Patricia Paylore and Donald M. Powell, we set about planning a regional conference on libraries in the Southwest, their rise, development and needs, to be held at Occidental in 1955, sponsored jointly by the Rockefeller Foundation and the California Library Association. Everything conspired to make it a success. Together with the Sacramento conference of 1950, the Occidental meeting was one of the most rewarding things I ever took part in.

Old Hodge was present and young Glen Dumke, the new Dean of the college. Erna Fergusson came from Albuquerque to speak on the rise of libraries in New Mexico. From retirement in Pasadena we brought Julia Brown Asplund, first professional librarian in New Mexico and organizer of that state's library extension service. Edwin Castagna spoke on the history of public libraries in the Southwest, Fernando Pesqueira on libraries of Sonora, Don Powell on Arizona library needs. The conference closed with my address on what a library school at UCLA could do for Southwestern library development and with the conference's peak of eloquence, Patricia Paylore's paper on "The Effect of Climate and Distance on Libraries in the Arid Regions."

Bookseller J. E. Reynolds reported the conference in the *Library Journal* under the heading "Low Barometer in the Southwest," and concluded:

> "When Dr. Powell finished his speech, twelve hours had passed since the opening of the conference. The average audience, after this length of time, would have expressed exhaustion both vocally and physically. Not this audience. There was exhilaration in the air to match the clear starlit sky that greeted the departing librarians as they left the hall. The barometer will soon be going up in the Southwest, of that you can be certain."

Reynolds's "soon" was a long five years.

The conference papers were issued in the UCLA Library Occasional Papers series and reprinted in 1960 when the Library School opened.

The only dissenting voice was that of an Oklahoman, Arthur McAnally, who never forgave me for calling his state marginally Southwestern—not until 1966, when I spoke twice in Oklahoma and smoked the peace pipe with Mac.

Starting in 1955 with *Heart of the Southwest*, I wrote a series of books which established my position as a lesser Dobie: *Books West Southwest*, essays published by Ritchie in a beautiful volume which, like his earlier format for *The Alchemy of Books*, was chosen by the American Institute of Graphic Arts as one of the Fifty Books of the Year; *A Southwestern Century*, my choice of the hundred best books of nonfiction which, together with *Heart of the Southwest*, appeared in *Arizona Highways*; *Libros Californianos*, a revision commissioned by Zeitlin of the earlier edition by Phil Townsend Hanna, and *Southwestern Book Trails, a Reader's Guide to the Heartland of Arizona and New Mexico*.

Inspired by Dobie, whom I called the finest Southwesterner of them all, I sought to reach reading travellers, travelling readers, and to relate literature to landscape. In bibliography, again following Dobie, I was selective, not comprehensive. Write more about fewer books, Dobie urged, and this I did, particularly in *Southwestern Book Trails*. To the Library's Occasional Papers, in addition to the Occidental Conference proceedings called *Libraries in the Southwest*, we added a compilation, *The Southwest of the Bookman*, essays by Dobie, Hertzog, Horn, Reynolds, Gjelsness, Paylore, and myself. Betty Rosenberg and I compiled a monthly checklist, *Books of the Southwest*, which attracted four hundred individual and library subscribers; and I continued to write my monthly column in *Westways*, which was widely used by libraries as a buying guide to books on the West.

This activity brought two invitations from Texas to conduct library surveys in and around Dallas and in San Antonio. The first was to recommend a program for the De Golyer Foundation, the richly endowed book collections formed by the late E. L. De Golyer, a pioneer petroleum geophysicist. I was asked to visit and evaluate the appropriate institutions of north Texas to determine which was best suited to house and administer the Foundation. In a week's time in the heat of August visits were paid to Baylor University at Waco, Texas Christian at Fort Worth, North Texas at Denton, and the Dallas Public Library and Southern Methodist University in Dallas. My written report favored S.M.U.

I was invited to return to Dallas, with Fay, and to elaborate orally on the report at a meeting of the Foundation's directors. This was held at a buffet dinner in the great bookroom of the De Golyer hacienda on the lakeshore east of Dallas. It was a memorable evening. The report was adopted, and today the De Golyer Foundation is located at Southern Methodist.

The second survey was on behalf of William Holman, City Librarian of San Antonio, who wanted recommendations for a special collections division in the Public Library. Bluebonnets along the runway, the Alamo and Mission San José, the Harry Hertzberg Circus Collection, formed the mosaic I took away with me.

In those years I spoke to library groups in Dallas, Austin, El Paso, San Antonio, and Houston, but except for El Paso and Dobie, and the quarterly *Southwest Review*, whose editors, Allen Maxwell and Margaret Hartley, had befriended my writing, I never admitted Texas into the innermost heart of the Southwest. Texas is Texas, a state unto itself, as every Texan proudly shouts.

I became identified with historical groups in Arizona, New Mexico, and California and was stimulated by their invitations to prepare and deliver some of my best work, moved by a sense of place and time and theme. "The Roots of Regional Literature" was given on a summer evening at New Mexico Highland University in Las

Vegas to an audience out-of-doors under great rustling cottonwoods. In it, I recalled that I had first come that way west on the Santa Fe Trail as an infant in my mother's arms. At Las Cruces, after being introduced by Senator Clinton Anderson, I spoke to the New Mexico Historical Society on "Act of Enchantment," in which I condemned Billy the Kid (the meeting was held in the heart of "badmen" country) and praised Popé, the Tewa Indian who led the Pueblo revolt of 1680. A write-up afterward in an El Paso newspaper gave me hell on both grounds.

An address to the Arizona History Conference in Tucson was called "Fountains in the Sand," in which I sought to embody my feelings about water in an arid land and to deplore the destruction of historical sites. This was also a theme of "The Sense of the Past," an address at the seventy-fifth anniversary of the Historical Society of Southern California. As president, my old colleague Gustave Arlt was in the chair that night.

In Berkeley, the Friends of the Bancroft Library annual lecture was called "Landscapes and Bookscapes of California." It recalled happy times in the Bancroft, when I had been a miserable library school student. At the Book Club of California's fiftieth anniversary banquet in San Francisco it was "The Prospect Before Us."

The elegiac vein came easily in the 1950's and early 1960's, as friend after friend died and I was called on to speak at memorial services. J. Gregg Layne, Phil Townsend Hanna, Robert Ernest Cowan, Henry R. Wagner, Regent Edward A. Dickson, Haniel Long, Frederick Webb Hodge, J. Frank Dobie, Erna Fergusson—one by one they went out of my life, and the links snapped that had bound me to the Southwest.

I began to sense a kind of cyclic fatality, and when in the spring of 1963 I wrote *Southwestern Book Trails* and its epilogue to the mountain ranges of New Mexico and Arizona, I knew fulfillment. Dedicated to Erna Fergusson and Patricia Paylore, native daughters of New Mexico, it was a farewell to the region. I have not returned since then to either state.

Several family deaths occurred in the 1950's, of my brother George in 1955 and my mother two years later. His was a blessing, for Edwina's death in 1953 had sounded his knell. He was sick and miserable and we had lost the ways of communication. My mother's death came a few months before her eighty-seventh birthday; she died in her sleep after the briefest illness. Her life had fulfilled itself. She had given all she could give to me, and she gave it without stint in the years of my greatest need. Fay and I placed her ashes, as she wished done, in Encinal Creek that flowed into the Pacific. I had copies printed in Holland of her manuscript *The Quiet Side of Europe*, a happy book about her years abroad, 1931–34, the crowning time of her life. No gravestone outlasts the memorial of a book. In it my mother lives, as it were, forever.

Sometime after 1955, I was in Albuquerque one furnace-hot summer morning; and browsing in the New Mexico Book Company's store, encountered Paul Horgan, whose Southwestern books I had included in my bibliographies. We repaired to the cool Franciscan Hotel next door and over tall glasses of iced coffee, we agreed on something that was to bring us back together in September 1960.

Knowing that Horgan had served as librarian of the New Mexico Military Institute in Roswell—an ideal job, he recalled, for it gave him time to write—I confided in him my dream of a library school at UCLA. When it would come true, I could not say, but when it did, I asked him if he would be the speaker at its dedication.

He replied ardently, "Indeed I will; ask me and I will come."

INTO THE PROMISED LAND

If my life between thirty and sixty were to be divided, the parts would be learning, doing, and teaching; and, as theme throughout, writing. When in 1944 Regent Dickson asked when I planned to open a school of the library, there was no thought other than to put him off. There was too much else to be done first. He was a stubborn man, however, and he never stopped pressing for an answer. As a member of the Los Angeles Public Library's Board of Commissioners, it galled him to see appointments going to graduates of USC's Library School.

If Mitchell had not retired, we might have developed a plan to extend the Berkeley school to UCLA, as he had begun to do in summer sessions during the late 1930's. But he had been succeeded as Dean by J. Periam Danton, a former Navy officer, who ran the school as he would a ship. By his brusque impersonality, and failure to travel about the state and reach librarians in the field, Danton lost the confidence of the school's alumni, and there were increasing demands to replace him. Students referred to the school as "Danton's Inferno." His chief efforts were

expended in persuading the Berkeley Senate to authorize
a doctoral program. It was a case of the mountain labor-
ing to bring forth a mouse: in the first ten years of the
doctoral program, the Berkeley school awarded one degree. Danton was honest, courageous, and a scholar in
the Germanic tradition, but he was not a good library
school administrator, and yet he held the office for fourteen years.

The Leigh survey, issued in 1952, recommended that
the Berkeley and USC schools expand and improve their
facilities, an obvious recommendation documented at
length by one who in his unfamiliarity with the political
facts of life in California had headquartered himself at
the State Library in Sacramento, as being neutral ground
between Berkeley and UCLA. It was not. Even under
Miss Gillis, the State Library was pro-Northern, and her
successor had no identification with cultural life south of
Tehachapi.

Leigh concluded that if the two schools did expand
and improve, a third school would not be necessary; but
if such were not the case, then UCLA was the logical
place for a new school. Then as a final point, he suggested that the USC school might transfer itself to
UCLA, as it had earlier received such a transfer from the
public library.

President Sproul is said to have asked the President of
USC if such a transfer would be considered and to have
received the reply that, as the weaker of the two schools,
Berkeley was a better prospect than USC for transfer to
UCLA.

Regent Dickson was furious, having opposed the survey from the beginning. Both Berkeley and USC played
possum. No expansion occurred at either school. I then
concluded that UCLA must have a school of its own,
and I set about rallying professional support for one. A
Board of Regents–State Department of Education task

force was preparing a Master Plan for Higher Education in California. By the mid-1950's it was near an end to the work. In my perennial optimism, I believed that it would recommend the establishment of a library school at UCLA. About the time of the Occidental Conference on the Southwest, we convened a group at UCLA to hear from professional sources of the need for a school. City and county chief librarians, university and school librarians, representing Southern California, Arizona and New Mexico were present, as was Regent Dickson and chairmen of key faculty committees, and the Dean of the Graduate Division. A summary memorandum followed. A breakthrough seemed imminent.

Then a twin setback occurred. The state's Master Plan for Higher Education appeared and recommended that no attention be given to a library school at UCLA for another five years, that is 1960, and Regent Dickson died. I must have a very thick skin. It didn't occur to me that I had been run through, knocked down, and put on the mortuary shelf.

I called a staff meeting and told them the sad news, and that I was nevertheless convinced of the need and intended to find new fronts on which to fight. I was in my office after the meeting, clearing my desk of the day's intake, when Everett Moore came in. He said that he and some of the staff believed that I had fought long enough by myself, and now they wanted to know how they could help. "Bravo!" I said. "Here's what we'll do."

Then was born what came to be known as the Library Education Seminar. For the next year about twenty of us met Monday evenings on a volunteer basis, not to study the need for a library school but rather to plan a new school—curriculum, faculty, and budget, in order to be ready when the time came to open. We invited speakers from different areas of librarianship, and to his credit, Dean Danton accepted our invitation to come down and tell us some of the problems we'd meet. According to him, the chief one would be in recruiting a faculty. We also invited Rudolph Gjelsness, Dean of the University of Michigan Library School, to come from Mexico City where he was on leave. Another educator who met with the seminar was Preben Kierkegaard, head of the Danish State Library School, who happened to come through Los Angeles. A dark Dane with a devilish beard, he fluttered every female heart on the staff.

All the while cries were heard from USC that Los Angeles could not support two library schools. I assigned Page Ackerman, aided by James Cox, to make a statistical study, which indicated that the heavily populated area of greater Los Angeles was not contributing its share per capita to the library profession; and for the reason that prospective students did not want to go 400 miles away to school at Berkeley; and that the tuition at the private USC was beyond their means. Only the presence in Los Angeles of a state-supported school would result in the recruitment so urgently needed to fill library vacancies throughout the state.

Miss Ackerman confessed afterward that she had undertaken the assignment unconvinced of the need for a UCLA school, but had ended as one of my strongest converts.

These were some of the means I used to fight the Leigh canard that the whole thing was merely my personal ambition. Ambition, yes, but professional, not personal. I already had all the authority, responsibility, and prestige I wanted. Fine feathers were not found on library school deans, nor did I sprout any after I became one.

The freeze until 1960 had riled two professional groups in Southern California in whose libraries there existed critical staff shortages: the Public Library Executives Association and the School Library Association. The latter had a militant spokesman on UCLA's behalf in the person of Elizabeth Neal, Librarian of Compton College. One day I was waited on by the "Big Three" of the PLEASC group: city librarians Hamill of Los Angeles and Castagna of Long Beach and county librarian Henderson of Los Angeles. Hamill literally pounded on the table and demanded to know when UCLA was going to start training librarians for his mounting vacancies.

"When you persuade the Regents to melt the freeze," was my reply.

I gave the same answer to Miss Neal.

Before long the Regents received resolutions passed by the membership of PLEASC and SLAC, requesting an immediate restudy of the need. The Regents acted. My old friend Tom Dabagh, on the President's research staff since leaving the UCLA law librarianship, and who in the meantime had served as executor of the Mitchell estate, was delegated to make the restudy. We gave him the facts and figures gathered by the seminar, and by Page Ackerman and James Cox. I was confident that a real need could be demonstrated. I had never forgotten Mitchell's last words to me: "There will be a school at UCLA if you can demonstrate the need for one."

On August 14, 1958, the Regents removed the 1960 barrier and approved a new school at the earliest possible date, setting as the only condition a limitation of fifty graduates for each of the first five years, as a kind of handicap to protect USC. And to add an element of Greek tragedy, Tom Dabagh died soon thereafter.

With Chancellor Raymond B. Allen's approval, I submitted a budget for a planning year 1959–60 and an opening in 1960–61. I had persuaded Andrew Horn to return to Southern California, after three years at North

Carolina, and he was serving as librarian of Occidental College, with an understanding between Dean Glen Dumke, Horn and me that he would be released to UCLA at such time as the new library school needed him. His and a secretary's salary were the chief items in the planning budget. Horn had given notice to Occidental and his replacement there appointed, when another catastrophe occurred. The Governor cut thirty-eight new programs from the university's budget. Ours was one of them. Page Ackerman phoned me the news at home one evening. I groaned, then growled, then thought, then slept.

In the morning I went to the Chancellor's office. Chancellor Allen had gone to Indonesia and physicist and former Dean of the Graduate Division Vern Knudsen was acting in his place. Knudsen not only knew Horn; he had been on his doctoral committee. He shared my indignation, and promised to fight for restoration of our budget. President Coons and Dean Dumke were amused by the failure of the university's usual legislative finesse.

I thought back to 1950 and the statewide friends I had made. One was now serving as the Governor's confidential secretary. I reached him by phone, and asked for his help.

Two of the thirty-eight deleted items were restored by the Governor. One was for an atomic energy project, sponsored by the College of Agriculture. The other was the UCLA Library School.

Had we reached the promised land? No. I now had to face the UCLA faculty. Its Senate committees were displeased by the way I had bypassed them in planning. Chancellor Allen was not available to tell them of the circumstances that had led him to authorize my procedure. The Budget Committee suggested that I resign as

University Librarian. They refused to recognize Horn
with a tenure appointment, which meant that for the
planning year he worked from the uncertain position of
lecturer.

I had assumed that I would serve as Dean, with Horn
as Associate Dean, and that I would continue as University Librarian for the first five years. I was eventually
grateful to the Budget Committee for refusing to en-
dorse this. They were not willing to forego the custom-
ary search procedure for a new Dean, to be appointed
July 1, 1960. So a faculty committee was set up and I
was requested to supply it with the names of prospects
for the deanship. I did so; and on his own, Horn gave
Knudsen a dossier on me, with supporting letters solic-
ited from library school deans and university librarians.
Horn went so far as to say that if I were not made Dean,
he would resign and go back to library work in the field.
And he meant it. There were volunteers for the deanship from various parts of the country, and Leigh wrote
from Columbia, where he had replaced White as Dean,
that UCLA might want White.

The committee proceeded with all deliberate speed to
take the better part of the academic year to do nothing,
and then in March of 1960 they recommended my
appointment as Dean. I learned, however, that they had
not included a professorial appointment, without which
the deanship alone was meaningless. I told the Acting
Chancellor that I could not accept one without the
other. An entirely new committee was set up, at the time
I took off on a flying trip to Japan and on to Europe. I
was on a mission to conduct an armed forces library
workshop in Tokyo on invitation of the Pacific Air
Force Command Librarian; and was flown afterward by
MATS to North Africa, from where I proceeded to
Rome.

By one of those turns of fortune, I found myself during a stopover in Hawaii at a luncheon given by the Hawaii Library Association, seated next to—Robert D. Leigh. He was in the new state to make a library survey. The news had come of my appointment as Dean. Leigh rose and offered congratulations. I responded with thanks to him for all he had done to bring about establishment of the new school. We shook hands to general applause. As politicians we had much in common.

The startling development of the spring of 1960 was Chancellor Allen's resignation and the appointment of Chancellor Franklin B. Murphy of the University of Kansas, Vosper's chief since he had gone to Lawrence in 1952.

Just before taking off for the Orient, I breakfasted at the Bel Air Hotel on invitation of Murphy, who was seeking advice from persons at UCLA as to his prospects if he accepted the chancellorship. It was my first meeting with the legendary bookman. I had heard from Vosper what a dynamic library supporter he was. During our initial talk, Murphy said that one of his hesitations in leaving Kansas was that he would be separated from Vosper. Then I played my ace. "I am serving as University Librarian only one more year. After July 1, 1961, I will be Dean of the School and Director of the Clark only."

"You are telling me that I need not be separated from Vosper?"

"The University Librarianship will be vacant on July 1 of next year."

"Which gives Vosper the necessary year to serve at Kansas after returning from his present sabbatical."

Then Murphy wanted to know whose appointment it was to make. I told him it was his, with faculty advice. Would the faculty so advise? I assured him that Vosper would be the overwhelming choice of the faculty to succeed me. Although he had been gone for eight years, they had never forgotten him.

And so it was. Acting Chancellor Knudsen appointed a committee; it met and swiftly recommended Vosper.

I was authorized by both Knudsen and Murphy to rendezvous with Vosper in Rome and carry the news of his selection. Murphy, still the Chancellor at Kansas, did not feel it ethical to enter at that time into any negotiations.

All went according to plan, although I knew anxious moments during the flight from Manila via Saigon, Bangkok, Calcutta, Karachi, and Dhahran. Due to connect with an Alitalia flight in Tripoli, I made it only as far as Cairo, where the C-121G came down on two of her four engines. Still my luck held. I got the last seat on a KLM flight to Rome, where I was met at the Ciampino airport by Bob and Loraine Vosper.

And here a few words about Loraine, one of the finest helpmeets a librarian ever had, willing and able to carry the social end of her husband's load, a cordial, humorous, vivacious woman of Swedish-Danish blood. Vosper and I were equally blessed in our wives.

We dined that night at a family restaurant in the Campo de Fiore, and the next morning at breakfast I told Vosper of Murphy's hope for a restoration of their partnership. He was naturally torn between loyalty to Kansas and a desire to return to UCLA. It was a tough decision that brought him back a year later as my successor.

I flew on to Zurich that same morning, relishing a cold zucchini salad on the Alitalia flight. There I found a cable from UCLA, telling of my appointment as professor, as well as dean, and transmitting an additional $20,000 in book funds. The lights were finally turning green.

Upon my return home the basic faculty was securely appointed, and on September 12, 1960, the school was dedicated by Chancellor Murphy, Dean Arlt, and Paul Horgan.

The latter's address, "One of the Quietest Things," was spoken from mind and heart. The audience held our first class, our faculty, and the friends who had helped us enter the promised land—and the friends who had not. I loved them all. Although Regent Dickson was dead, his widow rose and accepted the tribute voiced by Dean Arlt to the school's veritable grandfather. Thirty years and two months had passed since Edward Dickson first called for a "school of the library" at Westwood, and sixteen years since he had handed the task to me.

A BEGINNING AND END

"Powell has been a bad boy," it was said, "and for punishment he has been given a library school."

A sweet punishment it proved to be.

By 1960 UCLA was ready for library education, as it had not been in 1930, 1936, and 1944, those earlier times when Regent Dickson would have established a school if he had not been restrained successively by President Sproul, Librarian Goodwin (Dean Mitchell), and me.

In 1960 the UCLA campus was a mature university of arts, letters, and sciences, in undergraduate and graduate divisions and professional schools, supported by a central and branch library system. Around UCLA, in the greater Los Angeles area, was one of the country's best library networks, including public, academic, school, industrial, electronic, space age, and governmental operations. The region was ready for and entitled to the same kind of public-supported library education that the San Francisco Bay region had enjoyed since 1919.

From my own experience as a student at Berkeley, a teacher at Columbia, and an employer of graduates from a score of different American library schools, I had come to hold positive ideas on what a library school should and should not be. In speeches at home and abroad and in my writings, I had vigorously expressed these ideas, making friends and foes with equal gusto.

Now had come an opportunity to translate ideas into action. The local climate was favorable. Although USC was nervous, it never impeded our progress. At the 1955 Occidental conference I had said that the establishment of a library school at UCLA would help not hinder the school at USC, that it would increase not decrease their enrollment. This brought scornful laughter, but it came true. When it was apparent that the Trojan school would continue to flourish, Dean Martha Boaz relaxed, and we became cooperative and affectionate colleagues, visiting back and forth, speaking to one another's classes, and holding annual open houses each for the other's school. By her dedication and energy, she made her school a strong force in the library community.

The only open hostility was from a couple of members of the Southern California chapter of the Special Libraries Association, one of whom was the editor of the chapter publication. An issue of it appeared in which the UCLA school, then in its planning year, was attacked as inimical to USC. I was called a Communist.

Nothing came of it. The editor was replaced. We hosted the chapter later at a campus meeting, and I saw that the other disgruntled member, who had written to the Chancellor protesting our school, was given every courtesy.

If I was the spirit of the new school, Andrew Horn was the form. It was he who brought dream into reality. He provided the ground on which my feet were based. We were in essential agreement that the school would be bookish and humanistic, would emphasize bibliography, historical and applied, and would feature content rather than technique, the what and the why, rather than the how.

As a new graduate school in a research-oriented university, we were on thin ice. Many of our faculty colleagues in the older disciplines regarded librarianship as something less than a profession. The day after the school was announced in the press, I was asked by a colleague in the Faculty Club why I didn't take my trade school where it belonged, to California Polytechnic at San Luis Obispo. I allowed as how it was nice country up there, near Pismo Beach and the great sweep of sand dunes, but that we hoped to establish a school that would be a credit to the Graduate Division.

Horn was the one to do it. Trained in medieval history and classical languages, experienced as an assistant professor at the Johns Hopkins University, and as a library administrator at UCLA, North Carolina, and Occidental, he not only knew the academic ropes, he respected them. He punctiliously observed the rules, practices, and traditions of academic procedure at · UCLA, and proceeded to gain the support and admiration of the interdisciplinary advisory committee appointed by Chancellor Knudsen.

There was another problem which I had to meet. The profession at large, as I knew from my field work, believed that library education was too academic. Since Mitchell, Berkeley under Danton was regarded by many as an ivory tower. These very qualities that made Horn acceptable to our faculty, led garden-variety librarians to regard him as too academic. I helped offset this, but it was not until the library school faculty was completely assembled that our balance of theory and practice became evident.

In that first planning year 1959–60, I was deeply involved in my final term as University Librarian in the planning and funding of the new Research Library, conceived by Gordon Williams before he left to become director of the Midwest Inter-Library Center, and in an accelerated program at the Clark Library. In the year before Chancellor Murphy's arrival I was also embattled with an aggressive Senate Library Committee, demanding library parity with Berkeley, impossible of attainment without the local leadership eventually supplied by Murphy.

I learned that one man could not do justice to the librarianship and the deanship, and it was Horn that actually operated as dean in the year before we opened. He prepared information circulars in lieu of a printed catalog, outlined the core curriculum, answered more than five hundred inquiries from prospective students, and finally interviewed and admitted fifty as the first year's class. In all this he was aided by Ellie Schuetze, his winsome secretary (who later entered the school and received the M.L.S.), and by Barbara Boyd, a veteran county and state librarian I had persuaded to come to UCLA and take an M.A. in Public Administration, then join the faculty as our public library specialist. Horn also received generous aid from the library school at Berkeley.

My job was to pull Horn out of the depressions into which, as a pessimistic Scandinavian, he periodically slumped. Off campus we would go at noon. Double martinis for Andy, tonic water with a slice of lemon for me. I would infuse him anew with enthusiasm and away we would go on another round of what he described as petty triumphs and major defeats.

We were an indispensable, symbiotic pair, each fully aware and appreciative of the other's role and value. We never fell out. He was no yes-man. No one else could have done all that he did in the short year, against every bureaucratic and academic obstacle. A lesser man would not have endured the unjust treatment given him by the

Senate in refusing him initially a professorial appointment. Angry at me, they punished him. It was not until Chancellor Murphy showed his strength three years later that Horn was advanced to the professorship.

Another remarkable thing Horn did was to prepare himself better for teaching historical bibliography by learning from Saul Marks, Master of the Plantin Press, the rudiments of setting type and printing by hand. This led to the founding of the UCLA Library School Printing Chapel, in which students worked with Horn on noncredit printing projects, and also to an annual lecture series on Taste in Typography. This brought to campus Brooke Crutchley, printer to Cambridge University, Beatrice Warde of the Monotype Corporation, and Herman Zapf, the German calligrapher, as well as our own master printers, Saul Marks, Grant Dahlstrom, and Ward Ritchie.

Jake Zeitlin's long interest in all we did led to the establishment of the Zeitlin and Ver Brugge annual lectures on bibliography, given successively by F. N. Poynter, William A. Jackson, Sir Frank Francis, George Watson, Gordon N. Ray, and Fredson Bowers.

My interests attracted many bookish and literary visitors to the school, including Aldous Huxley, Paul Jordan-Smith, Kenneth Rexroth, Ray Bradbury, Robert Kirsch, Guy Endore, and Henry Miller. Our intention was to acquaint students with the creative people in the book world, and to encourage students after graduation to make their libraries centers of culture, not merely storehouses of books.

One of the most common criticisms of library education was that its teachers were too often undistinguished or incompetent librarians who had taken refuge on campus. I was determined that our faculty would be composed not only of teachers who could teach, could communicate, but who had also achieved recognition as outstanding librarians.

To this end I had an old pact with Frances Clarke Sayers, dean of children's librarians, equally noted as librarian, teacher, and writer. Upon her retirement from the New York Public Library, where she had directed the work with children, Mrs. Sayers joined the English Department at UCLA on a half-time basis, with the understanding that when it finally opened, the library school would have the other half of her time. It was my old friendship with Professor Ewing, now Chairman of the English Department, that helped bring this about.

When it finally came to pass, Frances Clarke Sayers brought to our students consummate knowledge, taste, passion. No one could enter her aura without being affected. In addition to teaching on campus, Mrs. Sayers spoke throughout the land. Before this great teacher's retirement in 1965, one of our students, Marjeanne Blinn, compiled a volume of Mrs. Sayers' writings, published by Viking as *Summoned by Books*, which won the author the Clarence Day Award. A year later she received the Joseph W. Lippincott Award for distinguished service to librarianship.

A similar pact was made with another national figure who joined the faculty in charge of cataloging and classification instruction. He was Seymour Lubetzky. I first met him when I came to UCLA in 1938. He had graduated from Berkeley with an M.A. in German and a library certificate, and was employed by Goodwin to enter periodicals in the card file, a task later assigned to student help. One day the head cataloger, Jens Nyholm, took Lubetzky and me to lunch and asked which of us would like to transfer to his department. He needed a man to talk with, he said. Lubetzky and I looked at each other. I shook my head. I knew my limitations and

201

interests, and confessed that I had barely made a C in cataloging. Lubetzky nodded his head. He had made an A. This transfer afforded him an escape from his menial assignment.

Lubetzky rose rapidly to be the chief classifier, and encouraged by Nyholm he contributed a series of searching and witty articles to the *Library Quarterly*. When Goodwin refused him the salary that went with his position, saying that seniority alone determined salaries, Lubetzky resigned and went to work in the Oakland shipyards. His work there was not entirely dissimilar to what he had done at UCLA, for he devised a classification scheme for shipbuilding parts and materials —rudders here, propellers there, and so on.

When Herman Henkle became head of technical processes in the Library of Congress he turned to his old mentor, Sydney Mitchell, for a classification specialist. Mitchell plucked Lubetzky from the shipyards and sent him to Washington. For the next eighteen years, with the encouragement of Luther H. Evans, Lubetzky became the mind and the voice of the catalog code revision and achieved international fame. At the same time he retained his wit and humor, his youthful mien, and his enormous vigor.

We kept in touch through the years, and when Lubetzky heard of my hope for a library school, he reported his readiness to return to UCLA as a member of our faculty. Although he had never taught a class since his earliest years in Poland as a school teacher, Lubetzky seemed to me a natural instructor, and so he proved to be.

Mrs. Sayers too had been on Goodwin's staff in the 1920's, as librarian of the University Elementary School. Thus it was a homecoming for her, Horn, and Lubetzky. As for me, I had never left the promised land, although the early pickins' had been mighty slim.

The three of them proved inspired and inspiring

teachers. With them alone, any school would have gained distinction. They were complemented by two lesser-known full-time teachers. Barbara Boyd, our public library instructor, and Betty Rosenberg, instructor in acquisitions, were members of the Berkely library school class of 1940, which also included Robert Vosper.

I first perceived Miss Boyd's teaching potential in 1956 at a campus institute on library administration, the proceedings of which appeared in the *Library Journal*. As a fellow member of one of the study groups into which the institute was divided, I was impressed by the cool and authoritative way she spoke. This is the kind of teacher she proved to be. She also served as a consultant to state, county, and city groups in need of library counsel.

Betty Rosenberg had been a member of my staff since 1946, lastly as my bibliographical assistant for book selection. She knew more about the writing, publishing, selling, collecting, and reading of books than any other librarian known to me; and she could communicate her knowledge with irreverent zest. Acquisitions to her was not what is commonly called a technical process; it was a way of life.

Part-time instruction in their special fields was offered by Robert Vosper, University Librarian and Professor of Library Service, in comparative librarianship; by Chase Dane, head of the Santa Monica school libraries, in school library work; and by Louise Darling in medical librarianship and Johanna Tallman in technological literature. As lecturer, Everett Moore gave occasional talks and advised on editorial matters. Elizabeth Baughman as assistant to Professor Lubetzky, Elizabeth Eisenbach as librarian of the school, and Florence Williams as administrative assistant to the dean, formed a trio of dedicated workers.

Because of the position I had frequently taken of

hostility toward the gadget worship of those librarians who were merely housekeepers—tinker-toy librarians I called them—our school was hardly expected to lead in data processing instruction. Yet this is what it did.

It was a year or more before the school opened that I had a visit from Robert M. Hayes, a rangy young UCLA Ph.D. in mathematics, who headed his own information systems company, affiliated with Hughes Aircraft. He told me that he had been asked by the UCLA Engineering-Mathematics Extension Department to teach a short course in data processing for libraries. Data processing he knew, having written his dissertation on computers, but in knowledge of libraries and their rise in the Western world he was deficient. What was the best way, he asked, of remedying this deficiency short of going to library school? This latter he was willing to do, but the course was to open a few weeks hence and he needed help fast.

Hayes impressed me as a man of strength and humility —identical qualities possessed by Andrew Horn, Seymour Lubetzky, and Frances Sayers. I sensed rather than saw his potential worth to us. I called Horn and Moore to my office and asked them to give Hayes a short course in traditional librarianship. They did, and he proved a swift learner.

After the school had opened I persuaded Hayes to serve as lecturer without salary, to advise us rather than to teach. Vosper induced him likewise to counsel the library on problems of automation. Raynard Swank, formerly librarian of Stanford University, had succeeded Danton as dean; and as members of the Library Council he and I collaborated with the university librarians in the establishment of an Institute for Library Research, of which Hayes ultimately became the director.

It was nervy of us to ask Hayes for so much free

advice, but he proved genial, generous, and patient, and loyal to his alma mater. In the meantime his local reputation became national as his book with Joseph Becker, *Information Storage and Retrieval*, proved a best seller. After we finally obtained his appointment as Professor of Library Service, with matching salary, we required our students to take his course in data processing. The school received approval of a parallel degree, Master of Science in Information Science. It was Horn, aided by Vosper, who steered this new program through channels.

Hayes, too, was a superb teacher, with split-second timing, a masterful expositor of the abstruse, a blackboard virtuoso, a humanistic mathematician in the great tradition going back to Euclid. I had no interest in data processing as such, or in any library housekeeping, but I knew enough to gather round me those who did and who were also humanists. Lubetzky, Hayes, and Horn were three such, possessed of analytic intellect, the power of lucid exposition, and the ability to communicate and persuade.

Perhaps my greatest triumph was in reconciling Frances Sayers wth Robert Hayes. Her disinterest in library technology eclipsed mine to the point of hostility toward the philistines who made library conferences deserts of dreariness. In the beginning, Hayes struck sparks from Sayers. Then, always the gentleman, he shrewdly asked her to recommend books for his own small son. That won her over. They ended by planning a conference on the effects of automation on children.

When Frances Sayers retired, the year before I did, we saluted her with a symposium on children's librarianship, addressed by Augusta Baker, her successor at the New York Public Library, Ruth Hill Viguers, editor of the *Horn Book*, Rosemary Livsey, head of children's work in the Los Angeles Public Library and my first boss there in 1937, and by Mae Durham, Mrs. Sayers' lively counterpart on the Berkeley faculty. Their papers were printed in Holland as *Come Hither*.

Mrs. Sayers' replacement shook the unperceptive library world as much as Lubetzky's and Hayes' appointments. Upon Vosper's initial suggestion, we brought Jerome Cushman from the New Orleans Public Library to fill the same split position between the school and the English Department. He was instantly successful as a teacher. With Barbara Boyd's return to field work, Cushman also became responsible for the public library courses.

From the opening semester, I carried my share of the teaching load. Except for a spring sabbatical in 1963, I taught both semesters and summer sessions of each year, 1960–66. The introductory course, advanced acquisitions, college and university library administration, and my special favorite, libraries and literature of the Southwest, were the courses for which I was responsible. My other chief activity was the interviewing of applicants. This I enjoyed almost as much as teaching.

The details of administration were skillfully and graciously handled by Florence Williams, the beautiful and wise Negro woman who had been with me since 1950. Throughout my career I had only two administrative assistants, Mrs. Williams and Miss Bradstreet, and I could write a book alone about what they did for me and for the people we served.

As Assistant Dean, Andrew Horn kept us in line with the Graduate Division. He and Mrs. Williams were responsible for the preparation of data required by the American Library Association's accreditation procedure. Accreditation came after the second year. The visiting team consisted of Eugene Wilson, Raynard Swank, and John S. Richards. They told us afterwards that impressive as the data were, it had been our students that had made the school outstanding.

Our six summer sessions were memorable because of the momentum attained by daily classes for six weeks, and because of the quality of the visiting faculty. These included Thomas Shaw of the Library of Congress; Roy Stokes from Loughborough Library School in England; Lewis Stieg, Librarian of the University of Southern California; Edwin Castagna of the Enoch Pratt Library; Richard Dillon of the Sutro Library; John D. Henderson, Los Angeles County Librarian; Theodore C. Hines of the School of Library Service at Columbia; and Joseph Shipman from the Linda Hall Library. All were superb teachers, and the students rocked and rolled under their impact.

Impact is the key word to what we sought to do, to hit the student with knowledge, to fire him with pride in the profession he was entering, imbue him with belief in the worth of library service, and to change him in the course of a year's study, in an atmosphere of humanistic bookishness. Each year we saw the bonds of affection formed between students themselves and between them and us. Graduation was a time of joyful, tearful, parting. Because the class was small and nearly all full-time, we came to know and to love our students. We of the faculty were determined to make the library school year one a student would always remember with pride and affection. I believe we succeeded. A teacher can have no better immortality than students who in turn become teachers, not necessarily in the formal sense.

The library school years from 1959, marked by the fulfillment of old hopes, were also climactic years for me as a speaker, traveller, and writer. The three books of essays published by Ward Ritchie—*Islands of Books, The Alchemy of Books,* and *Books West Southwest*—gained readers near and far, one of whom, William Targ, bookman and editor-in-chief of World Publishing Company, became my next advocate. Bearing the World imprint, three more books of essays and addresses—*A Passion for Books, Books in My Baggage*, and *The Little Package*—extended my influence even wider. Two of them were published also in England by Constable. These books proved good recruiting agents. Students were drawn to library work, and to UCLA in particular, by what I had written about the joys and the rewards of library service. A writer has no way of knowing how long his books will be read. That they were read in my time was enough for me.

The books also interested Francis Brown, editor of the *New York Times Book Review*, in my writings, and I became a frequent contributor of essays and reviews to that influential weekly. For the Thomas Y. Crowell Company's Poets series, edited by Lillian Morrison and Elizabeth Riley, I compiled a selection of Walt Whitman's poetry for young readers. By a strange and moving coincidence, I was pasting into the Whitman dummy the Lincoln elegy, "When Lilacs Last in the Dooryard Bloom'd," at the moment when the radio announced the assassination of President Kennedy.

For twenty years I had maintained a lively pace. Except for an occasional cold and a siege of iritis in 1958, after the rigors of the European trip, my health was excellent. Though I appeared frail, I was tough and resilient.

I cannot remember precisely when it was that I had the first thoughts of retiring before the mandatory age of sixty-seven. Gradually at first, then swiftly, I approached the decision to leave in 1966 at the time of my sixtieth birthday. Various reasons entered into the decision: I would probably live longer if my sixties were at a slower pace. I would have more time to write and thereby reach farther than the campus and the classroom. The ticked-off items in my ten-cent notebook indicated that I had done everything I had set out to do, and beyond this, it would only be repetitive. New vision and energy were needed for the rapidly developing electronic computer age, for the era of governmental aid to libraries. I was confident that Horn would succeed me just as ably as Vosper had done. They were two of the profession's best. I had always had a good sense of timing; now it told me to quit while I was ahead, to leave while I was still loved.

Early in 1964 I told Chancellor Murphy that I wished to retire two and a half years hence, and that I hoped Horn would be the new dean and Vosper the director of the Clark. Murphy was confident that both hopes would be realized. It meant that our income would be more than halved. Yet we had no sizable debts, and I figured on being able to earn more from my writing.

Then, the decision made, Fortune smiled. The death of my uncle, Harold Haines Clark, in March 1964, revealed me as an heir, with his widow Jessie and his sister Marian. He had in a way taken the place of my father. In my childhood he enthralled me with his story of "Aladdin and the Blue Monkey," and with the intricate pencilled mazes drawn on paper that he challenged me to thread my way out of. It was in his office, the Link-Belt Pacific Company, that I had worked as a dictaphone stenographer, and in his home that we had lived in that lean time between library school and library work. In his final illness—he too died as my mother did, six months short of his eighty-seventh birthday—I had comforted him in the hospital, seated by his bed, his hand in mine. As his executor, in the year it took to close the estate, I learned much about probate law and procedure.

As the time to retire approached, I felt the strength of the bonds that had to be broken: with the library school faculty and students; with the Clark Library staff with whom I had worked so closely and happily for nearly twenty-three years; with Chancellor Murphy who by his dynamic support had put the Clark into a higher orbit. And yet I knew the time had come. I had done all that I could do.

The university did not let me go unsung. Everett Moore arranged a Mozart concert at the Clark Library. The staff held a picnic for us. The Chancellor and his wife gave a steak broil, at which he and I held crackling dialogue, applauded by the Ritchies, the Zeitlins, the Horns, the Vospers, the Moores, and the Wilbur Smiths, some of those with whom we had come all the way.

Driving home afterward Fay and I recalled other old friends we would have wished to be there that night. Gordon Newell, living in Monterey and immersed in remunerative commissions for civic sculpture; Dr. Bieler, practicing medicine in Capistrano Beach and seeing his first book, *Food Is Your Best Medicine*, become a best seller; MacIntyre in Paris, paralyzed and bedridden, alas, the past six years; Georges Connes, living in retirement in Dijon and on his ancestral farm in the Rouergue where we had visited him on our sabbatical spring in 1963; Dr. Stelter, Dean Mitchell, Althea Warren, my mother, all dead these several years. All of them our indispensable friends, they and many others.

Andrew Horn and Florence Williams arranged a June convocation, with speeches, champagne, and luncheon, and a bibliography of my published writings compiled by Betty Rosenberg, prefaced by W. W. Robinson, and printed by Ward Ritchie. It was a gala affair, attended by 400 friends and colleagues, former staff members and students; and most touching of all, by President and Mrs. Sproul, the man who had given me the main chance, as big and almost as booming as ever. The speakers came from afar: James D. Hart, the scholarly bookman and printer from Berkeley, Philip M. Burnett, my former student, from Indiana University Library, and Neal

Harlow from Rutgers, where he is the dean of the library school. They were introduced by William Conway, my deputy at the Clark, by David Laird, president of the graduating class, and by Everett Moore. Chancellor Murphy and Librarian Vosper spoke after the buffet held in the old library.

Thirty-one years had passed since I first stood in the rotunda of that noble building and said to myself, "*This is the place.*" It was indeed the place to begin, the place to end. I did not know at the time that the Regents had named it the Lawrence Clark Powell Library, to be effective two months later at the actual date of my retirement, the date on which this book was begun.

Fortune had been with me throughout the swift years. She was still there. Was she smiling? One is never sure. My friends were surely there. And Fay, lovely and smiling. Enough for me.

AFTERWORD

Nearly a month has passed, as I wrote each day upon this version of my life. It is the first time in many years that I have been free to work in a regular, sustained way. Most all that I have written until now has been on the margins of a more than full-time job. The first draft came with a rush in a daily artesian flow. Now comes the revision and correction. It has been written without reference to notes or sources, from the head and the heart, with the hands—that triumvirate I liked to refer to as the basic elements of good librarianship.

I usually left the flat after breakfast, writing pad in my briefcase, and took the 29 bus to Charing Cross Road. In a Forte's coffee bar at the top of the Haymarket I enjoyed a *capucino*, then settled in at one of my two favorite writing places—the Westminster Central Reference Library in St. Martin's Street, or one of the rooms in the National Gallery on Trafalgar Square. The Rembrandt room was my preference, because of the settees and the self-portraits which showed what age had done to the painter. One morning a young woman sat down beside me and asked, "Are you an art critic?" "No," I replied, "but I know what I like."

Some mornings I would get off the bus at Victoria Station to watch departure of the *Golden Arrow*, then walk to Whitehall by way of Westminster Cathedral to see Eric Gill's Stations of the Cross.

Now that it is done, how can I judge either the living or the writing? Detached vision was not one of my gifts. If I had been given such, I would have stuck on dead center, appalled by what I saw, paralyzed by the consequences of my acts, particularly those before I achieved self-discipline.

A compulsion to create, to succeed, to be recognized and praised, moved me to do what I did, and yet I was never without the knowledge of what I owed to fortune and friendship. Wherever I went, whatever I did, I sacrificed to the gods. Whoever helped me, I tried in turn to help; or if he did not need it, then I sought to help someone else in need. This law of compensation I tried always to honor, and in my teaching to impress it on my students. If one has been helped, then he must help others. If he has received, then he must give. Only by unloading some of what he has, can one make room for more.

I never hated anyone, or sought to hurt anyone, nor did I have a troubling conscience. Once self-mastery and health were gained, I ate well, eliminated regularly, slept deeply and awoke refreshed. Health for me lay in action, not in reflection. The things that came hardest were the best. My fault was that too often I was satisfied with easy success. This led to ham acting, to plays for the obvious laugh. I was guilty also of the slapdash, the superficial, and of too much hyperbolic utterance.

I hope now to escape some of these faults and limitations, and to live a simpler, purer life, and to write better. Perhaps even to be reflective. I can only hope.

There is limited escape from one's time and one's self. I never used energy in war with myself. When in 1953 I paid my first visit to Haniel Long, the sage of Santa Fe, he inscribed a copy of his *Walt Whitman and the Springs of Courage* with these words of Whitman, words which I took thereafter as a kind of talismanic epigraph to my own life: "Reconciliation, word over all, beautiful as the sky." There is a difference between self-reconciliation and self-satisfaction.

The weather has remained fine throughout September. All we had to do was to buy an umbrella. Since then not a drop has fallen. Reverse rain medicine.

I have not spent all of the time in writing. We have revisited favorite haunts—the Wallace and the Courtauld collections, the Royal Hospital grounds in Chelsea, Soho for Irish soda bread. We have also been to Festival Hall to hear the Menuhins play Beethoven sonatas, to Covent Garden for a Russian ballet's *Cinderella* and *Petrouchka*, to Wigmore Hall where a trio of young Americans played Mozart and Dohnanyi. Deep in Berkshire we have visited my beloved niece Marcia, Clark's daughter, long married to Captain Guy Lawrence and blessed with three children. In London we have seen our old friends Winifred Myers, Netta Aldington, Sir Frank and Lady Francis, Stanley and Sally Smith, Alan and Ella Thomas, Harold and Olive Edwards, Ruth Collis, and Trevor Brown. One evening we stood on the Embankment here in Pimlico and watched a River festival on the 300th anniversary of the Great Fire.

Now the smoke from Battersea's stacks rises into the windless sky. The autumn equinox has passed. It is tea time. Fay fills my cup. It all but runneth over.

Rodney House
Dolphin Square
London, S. W. 1

INDEX

215

217